Contents

Useful facts and figures

Hamlyn all-colour cookbooks

Salads and Vegetables

Marguerite Patten

Hamlyn
London · New York · Sydney · Toronto

Published by
The Hamlyn Publishing Group Limited
London · New York · Sydney · Toronto
Astronaut House, Feltham, Middlesex, England
© Copyright The Hamlyn Publishing Group Limited 1973
ISBN 0 600 30212 1
Printed in England by Sir Joseph Causton and Sons Limited
Line drawings by John Scott Martin
Set 'Monophoto' by Page Bros (Norwich) Limited

Note on metrication

In this book quantities are given in both Imperial and metric measures. Exact conversion from Imperial to metric does not always give very convenient working quantities so for greater convenience and ease of working we have taken an equivalent of 25 grammes/millilitres to the ounce/fluid ounce. 1 oz. is exactly 28·35 g. and $\frac{1}{4}$ pint (5 fl. oz.) is 142 ml., so you will see that by using the unit of 25 you will get a slightly smaller result than the Imperial measures would give.

Occasionally, for example in a basic recipe such as a Victoria sandwich made with 4 oz. flour, butter and sugar and 2 eggs, we have rounded the conversion up to give a more generous result. For larger amounts where the exact conversion is not critical, for instance in soups or stews, we have used kilogrammes and fractions (1 kg. equals 2·2 lb.) and litres and fractions (1 litre equals 1·76 pints). All recipes have been individually converted so that each recipe preserves the correct proportions.

Oven temperatures

The following chart gives the Celsius (Centigrade) equivalents recommended by the Electricity Council.

Description	Fahrenheit	Celsius	Gas Mark
Very cool	225	110	$\frac{1}{4}$
	250	130	$\frac{1}{2}$
Cool	275	140	1
	300	150	2
Moderate	325	170	3
	350	180	4
Moderately hot	375	190	5
	400	200	6
Hot	425	220	7
	450	230	8
Very hot	475	240	9

Introduction

We are very fortunate in this country in that we have such an excellent selection of home-grown vegetables throughout the year. In addition we import many of the more exotic vegetables from other parts of the world. This means we can produce an almost unlimited variety of salads and vegetable dishes from January to December.

Many of the recipes in this book will appeal to those of you who are vegetarians; but in addition you will find vegetables combined with meat and fish to give colourful, appetising and nutritious main dishes. So many people of all ages are anxious to lose weight, or maintain a slim figure; if you are among this number then some of the dishes in this book are designed for that particular purpose; they are low in calories and carbohydrates, but provide satisfying meals.

I think most cooks agree that coloured photographs of the finished dishes are an incentive to try the recipes, and I always enjoy looking at pictures of salads and vegetables, for they emphasise the important fact that eye-appeal plays an essential part in cookery and nature has provided an abundance of colourful ingredients in every kind of vegetable.

Try to incorporate an unexpected touch in your salads, such as using raw mushrooms (see page 12), adding fruit to the more familiar ingredients (see pages 10 and 28), etc.

A diet that contains plenty of fresh salads and carefully cooked vegetables helps to maintain good health, and that is important for all of us.

Coleslaws

Preparation time: 10 minutes
Main utensil: mixing bowl
Each salad serves: 6–8

Carrot coleslaw

Imperial
1 small white cabbage
4–6 large carrots
coleslaw dressing (see note)

Metric
1 small white cabbage
4–6 large carrots
coleslaw dressing (see note)

1. Remove the outer leaves from the cabbage, then cut it into portions and soak for a short time in cold water. Drain and dry well, shred very finely. Peel and grate the carrots coarsely.
2. Blend the cabbage and carrots together, toss in dressing until thoroughly moistened, allow to stand for 30 minutes.

Apple coleslaw

Imperial
4–6 sticks celery, finely chopped
3 dessert apples, peeled and
    thinly sliced
4 oz. sultanas
4 oz. chopped walnuts
1 small white cabbage
blue cheese dressing (see note)

Metric
4–6 sticks celery, finely chopped
3 dessert apples, peeled and
    thinly sliced
100 g. sultanas
100 g. chopped walnuts
1 small white cabbage
blue cheese dressing (see note)

Blend the first four ingredients together, add to the finely shredded cabbage and mix with the dressing, stand for 1 hour.

Virginia coleslaw

Imperial
½ small white cabbage
½ small red cabbage
¼ medium-sized cucumber
1 small green pepper
3–4 sticks celery
4 medium-sized carrots
1 small onion
coleslaw dressing (see note)

Metric
½ small white cabbage
½ small red cabbage
¼ medium-sized cucumber
1 small green pepper
3–4 sticks celery
4 medium-sized carrots
1 small onion
coleslaw dressing (see note)

1. Shred the cabbages, dice the other vegetables, except the carrots and onion, which should be finely chopped or grated.
2. Add the dressing and mix all well together. Stand for 1 hour.

Note: Alternatively, flavour mayonnaise with a little extra sugar, mixed spice and tarragon or tarragon vinegar. For blue cheese dressing flavour mayonnaise with crumbled blue cheese.

Cabbage rose salad

Preparation time: 15 minutes
Main utensil: mixing bowl
Serves: 8–10

Imperial	Metric
1 large red cabbage	1 large red cabbage
1 small white cabbage	1 small white cabbage
2 grapefruit	2 grapefruit
2 dessert apples	2 dessert apples
4 oz. celeriac or celery	100 g. celeriac or celery
$\frac{1}{4}$ pint mayonnaise (see page 27)	125 ml. mayonnaise (see page 27)
$\frac{1}{4}$ pint sour cream	125 ml. sour cream
2 oz. pecan nuts, walnuts or hazelnuts	50 g. pecan nuts, walnuts or hazelnuts
2 red peppers	2 red peppers

1. Remove the outside leaves from the red cabbage, cut the stalk down to the base of the leaves.

2. Fold back the next two layers of leaves and cut out the centre of the cabbage. This can be cooked as an accompaniment for another meal.

3. Wash the shell in cold water, drain well.

4. Shred the white cabbage finely, wash it well, drain and then dry thoroughly.

5. Cut away the skin and pith from the grapefruit and dice the flesh.

6. Core but do not peel the apples; dice.

7. Peel the celeriac, grate coarsely or shred finely, or chop the celery.

8. Blend the vegetables with the mayonnaise and sour cream, add the nuts and fruit.

9. Discard the core and seeds from the red peppers. Shred the flesh and blend most of it with the salad, save a little for garnish.

10. Pile the salad into the red cabbage shell. Top with a little red pepper.

Mushroom and pepper salad

Preparation time: 10 minutes
Main utensils: screw-topped jar, salad bowl
Serves: 4–5

Imperial	Metric
Dressing:	*Dressing:*
4 tablespoons olive oil	4 tablespoons olive oil
juice of 1 lemon	juice of 1 lemon
pinch celery salt	pinch celery salt
shake pepper	shake pepper
good pinch salt	good pinch salt
pinch dry mustard	pinch dry mustard
1 tablespoon chopped parsley	1 tablespoon chopped parsley
Salad:	*Salad:*
1 large green pepper	1 large green pepper
1 large red pepper	1 large red pepper
2 large firm tomatoes	2 large firm tomatoes
8 oz. button mushrooms	200 g. button mushrooms
1 can anchovy fillets	1 can anchovy fillets

1. Blend the ingredients for the dressing together. A screw-topped jar is a good way of doing this; put the ingredients into the jar and shake firmly.

2. Remove the seeds from the red and green peppers. Cut the flesh into narrow strips.

3. Skin the tomatoes; this can be done by putting them into boiling water for 1 minute, then into cold water, or by inserting a fine skewer into the tomato and holding it over heat until the skin breaks.

4. Chop the tomatoes. Wash and slice some of the mushrooms, keeping some whole.

5. Toss the vegetables in the dressing. Arrange in a bowl, and garnish with anchovies.

6. Serve as an hors d'oeuvre or with meat or fish.

Celeriac salad with cream cheese dressing

Preparation time: 20 minutes
Main utensil: small mixing bowl
Serves: 4

Imperial	Metric
2 large celeriac	2 large celeriac
4 oz. cream cheese and	100 g. cream cheese and
2 oz. Cheddar cheese or	50 g. Cheddar cheese or
2 oz. Camembert	50 g. Camembert
$\frac{1}{4}$ pint mayonnaise (see page 27)	125 ml. mayonnaise (see page 27)
1 tablespoon lemon juice	1 tablespoon lemon juice
2 tablespoons thin cream	2 tablespoons thin cream
Garnish:	*Garnish:*
black olives	black olives
celery leaves or watercress	celery leaves or watercress
(optional)	(optional)
parsley	parsley

1. Peel the celeriac and grate or cut into matchsticks. Leave it in a bowl of cold water to which a little vinegar has been added whilst preparing the dressing, this prevents discolouration.

2. Put the cream cheese into a bowl. Add the finely grated Cheddar cheese or the Camembert, and beat well.

3. Gradually blend in the mayonnaise, add the lemon juice and cream.

4. Drain the celeriac carefully, mix it well with the dressing and pile it on to a serving dish. Garnish the salad with black olives, chopped parsley and celery leaves or watercress.

Variation

Use all cream cheese instead of a mixture of cream cheese and Cheddar or Camembert. The celeriac can be cut into matchsticks and cooked in boiling salted water until just tender. Drain, chill and serve mixed with a piquant mayonnaise.

Meat salad

Preparation time: 15 minutes plus time to stand
Main utensil: mixing bowl
Serves: 4

Imperial	Metric
4 oz. cooked beef	100 g. cooked beef
8 oz. cooked ham or pork	200 g. cooked ham or pork
4 oz. cooked, stoned prunes	100 g. cooked, stoned prunes
8 anchovy fillets	8 anchovy fillets
8 small pickled onions	8 small pickled onions
Horseradish dressing:	*Horseradish dressing:*
2 teaspoons grated fresh horseradish	2 teaspoons grated fresh horseradish
$\frac{1}{2}$ teaspoon dry mustard	$\frac{1}{2}$ teaspoon dry mustard
good pinch salt	good pinch salt
shake pepper	shake pepper
1 tablespoon lemon juice or vinegar	1 tablespoon lemon juice or vinegar
2 tablespoons concentrated tomato purée	2 tablespoons concentrated tomato purée
1 tablespoon chopped parsley	1 tablespoon chopped parsley
Garnish:	*Garnish:*
lettuce	lettuce
1 orange	1 orange

1. Dice the meat neatly and mix it with the diced prunes, the chopped anchovy fillets and halved onions.

2. Blend all the ingredients for the dressing together.

3. Mix with the meat mixture and allow to stand for about 1 hour so that the meat will absorb the flavour of the dressing. (Cover well to prevent drying.)

4. Arrange the lettuce on a long dish with the meat mixture down the centre.

5. Garnish with twists of orange. Serve as cold as possible. If putting in the refrigerator, cover well to keep the meat moist.

Slimmers' salad

Preparation time: 20 minutes
Main utensil: sharp knife
Serves: 4

Imperial	Metric
8 medium-sized tomatoes	8 medium-sized tomatoes
8 oz. cottage cheese	200 g. cottage cheese
4 anchovy fillets	4 anchovy fillets
4 sliced, stuffed olives	4 sliced, stuffed olives
1 carrot	1 carrot
2 sticks celery	2 sticks celery
lettuce leaves	lettuce leaves
2 tablespoons sour cream	2 tablespoons sour cream
few drops tomato ketchup	few drops tomato ketchup
2 teaspoons lemon juice	2 teaspoons lemon juice
pepper	pepper
2 oz. prawns	50 g. prawns
Garnish:	*Garnish:*
paprika pepper	paprika pepper

1. Remove the top from each tomato, scoop out and reserve the seeds and some of the pulp.
2. Stuff the cavity with cottage cheese and chopped anchovy fillets.
3. Top with 2 slices stuffed olives.
4. Place the tomatoes in an hors d'oeuvre dish.
5. Cut the carrot into sticks and slice the celery thinly.
6. Put these into a bowl of iced water to form curls, then arrange on the dish.
7. Arrange the lettuce leaves on a dish for the prawns.
8. Blend together the sour cream, tomato pulp (from stage 1), tomato ketchup, lemon juice and pepper.
9. Blend in the prawns and pile on top of the lettuce just before serving.
10. Sprinkle over a little paprika pepper for garnish. Serve either as an hors d'oeuvre or as a light main course.

Note: Each serving contains approximately 140 calories.

Variation
Use flaked cooked fish or finely chopped onion instead of anchovy fillets.

Salmon mayonnaise

Preparation time: 15 minutes
Main utensils: 2 mixing bowls
Serves: 4

Imperial	Metric
10 oz. cooked or well-drained canned salmon	250 g. cooked or well-drained canned salmon
3 medium-sized firm tomatoes	3 medium-sized firm tomatoes
about 3 inches cucumber	about 8 cm. cucumber
4 oz. cooked peas	100 g. cooked peas
4 oz. cooked potatoes (preferably new)	100 g. cooked potatoes (preferably new)
Dressing:	*Dressing:*
2 tablespoons mayonnaise (see page 27)	2 tablespoons mayonnaise (see page 27)
1 tablespoon lemon juice	1 tablespoon lemon juice
pinch sugar	pinch sugar
pinch salt	pinch salt
shake pepper	shake pepper
2 teaspoons chopped dill	2 teaspoons chopped dill
Garnish:	*Garnish:*
1 lettuce	1 lettuce
1 hard-boiled egg	1 hard-boiled egg

1. Flake the fish and put it into a bowl.
2. Skin the tomatoes and dice neatly; blend with the salmon.
3. Peel and dice the cucumber finely, add to the fish together with the peas and diced potatoes.
4. Make the dressing by blending the mayonnaise with the other ingredients.
5. Spoon over the fish mixture, mixing gently until moist.
6. Shred most of the lettuce in a bowl, pile the fish mixture on top of this and garnish with a ring of shredded lettuce, then a flower design of quartered hard-boiled egg. Alternatively, serve in small individual salad bowls.

Variations
Add a little chopped chives to dressing. Mix the salmon with prawns or other shellfish. Blend chopped hard-boiled egg into the salad with the fish.
Egg mayonnaise: Hard boil eggs and arrange them on a bed of lettuce. Coat with the mayonnaise dressing, omitting the dill. Sprinkle with paprika and garnish with prawns and watercress if liked (see front cover).

Fish salad

Preparation time: 20 minutes
Main utensil: mixing bowl
Serves: 4

Imperial	Metric
Sharp sauce:	*Sharp sauce:*
1 tablespoon dry mustard	1 tablespoon dry mustard
1 tablespoon sugar	1 tablespoon sugar
1 tablespoon lemon juice	1 tablespoon lemon juice
grated rind of 1 lemon	grated rind of 1 lemon
5 tablespoons wine vinegar	5 tablespoons wine vinegar
1 small onion	1 small onion
good pinch cayenne pepper	good pinch cayenne pepper
good pinch salt	good pinch salt
few drops Tabasco sauce	few drops Tabasco sauce
2 tablespoons chopped dill	2 tablespoons chopped dill
Salad:	*Salad:*
12 oz. cooked white fish	300 g. cooked white fish
2 oz. shelled prawns	50 g. shelled prawns
4 oz. cooked or canned peas	100 g. cooked or canned peas
2 hard-boiled eggs, sliced	2 hard-boiled eggs, sliced
1 medium-sized cooked beetroot, diced	1 medium-sized cooked beetroot, diced
1 lettuce	1 lettuce
Garnish:	*Garnish:*
cucumber slices	cucumber slices
few unshelled prawns	few unshelled prawns

1. Make the sauce by blending all the ingredients together in a basin or by shaking them together in a screw-topped jar — the onion should be crushed and the juice only used.

2. Flake the fish and blend with the prawns and the dressing. If wished, a little less of the sharp sauce may be used to give a slightly less moist salad.

3. Add the peas, sliced eggs and diced beetroot.

4. Pile neatly on to a bed of crisp lettuce.

5. Garnish with cucumber slices and prawns. Serve really cold.

Variation

Use canned tuna or salmon instead of white fish, or use a mixture of shell and white fish, cockles or mussels are excellent.

Beetroot salad

Preparation time: 10 minutes
Main utensil: basin
Serves: 4

Imperial	Metric
2 cooked beetroots	2 cooked beetroots
½ pint sour cream	250 ml. sour cream
1 egg yolk	1 egg yolk
1 teaspoon made mustard	1 teaspoon made mustard
seasoning	seasoning
Garnish:	*Garnish:*
chopped parsley	chopped parsley

1. Peel the beetroots and cut them into large cubes.

2. Blend the sour cream into the well-beaten egg yolk, add the mustard and seasoning.

3. Pile the beetroot on to a serving dish and spoon over the dressing. Garnish with chopped parsley. Serve chilled as an accompaniment to cold meats.

Variation

Add diced cooked new potatoes, and cooked haricot or broad beans to the beetroot. Make a dressing of 6 oz (150 g.) cream cheese gradually blended with ¼ pint (125 ml.) mayonnaise (see next recipe), a little lemon juice, a little horseradish and 2 tablespoons thin cream. Mix the vegetables with the dressing, garnish with strips of gherkin or green pepper.

Ham and green pea salad

Cooking time: 20 minutes
Preparation time: 20 minutes
Main cooking utensil: saucepan
Serves: 4–5

Imperial	Metric
1¼–1½ lb. peas or equivalent in frozen or canned peas	½–¾ kg. peas or equivalent in frozen or canned peas
sprig mint	sprig mint
pinch sugar	pinch sugar
seasoning	seasoning
2 tablespoons mayonnaise (see below)	2 tablespoons mayonnaise (see below)
1 medium-sized cucumber	1 medium-sized cucumber
6–8 oz. cooked ham	150–200 g. cooked ham
3 tablespoons oil	3 tablespoons oil
1½ tablespoons white wine vinegar	1½ tablespoons white wine vinegar
Garnish:	*Garnish:*
cucumber	cucumber
mayonnaise	mayonnaise
parsley	parsley

1. Shell the peas and put them into boiling water with the mint, sugar and seasoning.
2. Cook steadily until they are tender; meanwhile prepare the other ingredients.
3. Make the mayonnaise (see below).
4. Cut off about 12 slices of cucumber, retaining the skin.
5. Peel and dice the remaining cucumber.
6. Dice the ham, keeping back a small amount, and cut this into triangles for garnish.
7. Blend the oil, vinegar and mayonnaise together to give a thin piquant dressing, toss the hot peas, diced cucumber and ham in this.
8. Pile the mixture into the centre of the dish with the triangles of ham and sliced cucumber round, and a few slices on top.
9. Garnish with piped mayonnaise and parsley. Serve as a light main dish with a bowl of crisp lettuce.

To make mayonnaise: Blend an egg yolk with a pinch of salt, pepper, mustard and sugar. Add about 1 teaspoon vinegar or lemon juice, then gradually blend in about ¼ pint (125 ml.) oil drop by drop, beating well with a wooden spoon.

Californian stuffed celery and Stuffed prune salad

Cooking time: 1 hour
Preparation time: 10 minutes plus time for prunes to soak, if necessary
Main cooking utensils: steamer, or basin and saucepan
Each salad serves: 6–12 people (depending upon other accompanying light dishes)

Californian stuffed celery

Imperial
4–6 prunes
1 large head celery
4 oz. cream cheese
2 oz. grated Cheddar or
    Parmesan cheese
seasoning
2 tablespoons mayonnaise
    (see page 27, optional)

Metric
100–150 g. prunes
1 large head celery
100 g. cream cheese
50 g. grated Cheddar or
    Parmesan cheese
seasoning
2 tablespoons mayonnaise
    (see page 27, optional)

1. Soak the prunes overnight, then steam in a steamer or basin over boiling water for 1 hour, which makes them firmer than simmering in liquid. Remove the stones; this and steaming may be unnecessary today as one can buy pitted (stoned) pre-tenderised prunes.
2. Cut the top off the celery, take a few young leaves, chop these finely to add to the cheese mixture.
3. To stuff the whole celery head, pull the sticks away, wash thoroughly. Blend the cream cheese, grated cheese, seasoning and chopped prunes together. Add the mayonnaise and the chopped celery leaves.
4. Press the mixture into each stick, then re-assemble the celery head. Leave to chill, then slice across.

Stuffed prune salad

Imperial
4–6 oz. prunes
1 large head celery
4 oz. Danish blue cheese
2 oz. cream cheese
2 oz. walnuts (optional)

Metric
100–150 g. prunes
1 large head celery
100 g. Danish blue cheese
50 g. cream cheese
50 g. walnuts (optional)

1. Prepare the prunes as above. Wash the celery sticks, blend the cheeses with the chopped nuts.
2. Pile the mixture into the sticks, cut into convenient lengths. Garnish with the prunes.

Leek salad

Cooking time: 15–20 minutes
Preparation time: 15 minutes
Main cooking utensil: saucepan
Serves: 4

Imperial	Metric
8 young leeks	8 young leeks
Dressing:	*Dressing:*
4 tablespoons oil	4 tablespoons oil
1½ tablespoons vinegar or lemon juice	1½ tablespoons vinegar or lemon juice
seasoning	seasoning
Garnish:	*Garnish:*
2–3 tablespoons chopped parsley	2–3 tablespoons chopped parsley
4 oz. coarsely grated cheese, Mozzarella or Bel Paese if possible	100 g. coarsely grated cheese, Mozzarella or Bel Paese if possible

1. Wash the leeks and cut them into equal lengths.
2. Cook in boiling salted water until just tender, do not overcook for they must have quite a firm texture.
3. Make the dressing by blending the oil, vinegar and seasoning together.
4. Cool the leeks, then toss in the dressing.
5. Lift out of the dressing and arrange them on a shallow dish.
6. Garnish with bands of chopped parsley and coarsely grated cheese. Serve as a light main dish or an antipasto (hors d'oeuvre).

Variation
Shred a green pepper and a small well-washed fennel root finely. Slice the leeks finely before cooking. Cook till barely tender, drain, mix with the pepper and fennel and toss in the oil and vinegar. Serve piled on a bed of lettuce.

Beetroot and ham salad

Cooking time: 10 minutes
Preparation time: 15 minutes
Main cooking utensil: saucepan
Serves: 4–6

Imperial	Metric
3 eggs	3 eggs
2 medium-sized cooked beetroots	2 medium-sized cooked beetroots
1–2 tablespoons oil	1–2 tablespoons oil
1 tablespoon vinegar	1 tablespoon vinegar
seasoning	seasoning
1–2 dessert apples	1–2 dessert apples
4–6 oz. cooked ham	100–150 g. cooked ham
lettuce	lettuce
Garnish:	*Garnish:*
1 lemon	1 lemon
few cocktail onions and/or olives	few cocktail onions and/or olives

1. Hard boil the eggs, crack the shells; keep one egg for garnish.
2. Halve the other two eggs, remove the yolks, chop the yolks and whites separately; do not chop too finely.
3. Peel and cut the beetroots in slices, then in matchsticks.
4. Put these into a bowl with the oil, vinegar and seasoning.
5. Peel the apples, cut them into neat pieces and add to the beetroot with the diced ham.
6. Mix the egg yolks and whites with the beetroot, pile on to a bed of lettuce.
7. Garnish with rings of hard-boiled egg, lemon and the onions and/or olives.
8. Serve with fresh bread or rolls. This also makes an excellent hors d'oeuvre for 6–8 people, particularly good if fish is the main course.

Variation

Omit the apple, add cooked rice or diced cooked potato.

Japanese salads

Cooking time: first recipe no cooking, second recipe few minutes
Preparation time: 15 minutes
Main cooking utensil: saucepan
Each salad serves: 4

Pineapple and pepper

Imperial
2 rings pineapple, cubed
1 eating apple, cored and sliced
juice of $\frac{1}{2}$ lemon
watercress
$\frac{1}{2}$ red pepper, sliced
$\frac{1}{2}$ green pepper, sliced
1 oz. peeled prawns
2 whole prawns

Metric
2 rings pineapple, cubed
1 eating apple, cored and sliced
juice of $\frac{1}{2}$ lemon
watercress
$\frac{1}{2}$ red pepper, sliced
$\frac{1}{2}$ green pepper, sliced
100 g. peeled prawns
2 whole prawns

1. Arrange a semicircle of pineapple on a dish.
2. Complete the circle with apple slices soaked in lemon juice.
3. Garnish with watercress, where the apples and pineapple meet.
4. Form a second semicircle with slices of red pepper, complete with green pepper.
5. Fill the centre with peeled prawns and garnish with whole prawns.

Prawn and pear dessert

Imperial
1 pear
juice of $\frac{1}{2}$ lemon
1 teaspoon castor sugar
1 tablespoon water
1 oz. cooked haricot beans
2 oz. peeled prawns
parsley
6 lichees
4 whole prawns

Metric
1 pear
juice of $\frac{1}{2}$ lemon
1 teaspoon castor sugar
1 tablespoon water
25 g. cooked haricot beans
50 g. peeled prawns
parsley
6 lichees
4 whole prawns

1. Simmer the peeled sliced pear in lemon juice, castor sugar and water for a few minutes, then drain and chill.
2. Arrange a semicircle of haricot beans around the side of a dish.
3. Add the prawns, garnish with parsley.
4. Arrange another circle of the pear slices, and well drained canned or shelled fresh lichees.
5. Fill with prawns. Serve with cream cheese flavoured with soy sauce and ginger.

Cauliflower salad

Cooking time: 10 minutes
Preparation time: 20 minutes
Main cooking utensil: saucepan
Serves: 4

Imperial	Metric
1 medium-sized cauliflower	1 medium-sized cauliflower
1 tablespoon vinegar	1 tablespoon vinegar
2 tablespoons oil	2 tablespoons oil
seasoning	seasoning
2 teaspoons chopped chives	2 teaspoons chopped chives
¼ pint mayonnaise	125 ml. mayonnaise
(see page 27)	(see page 27)
lettuce	lettuce
Garnish :	*Garnish :*
2 hard-boiled eggs	2 hard-boiled eggs
2 tomatoes	2 tomatoes

1. Wash the cauliflower thoroughly and divide it into sprigs. Cook in boiling salted water until just tender. Drain well.
2. Mix the vinegar, oil and seasoning together and toss the cauliflower in this whilst still warm. This helps to keep it moist.
3. Whilst the cauliflower is cooling prepare the mayonnaise.
4. Pile the cauliflower on a bed of lettuce and sprinkle with chives. Garnish with the mayonnaise, quartered hard-boiled eggs and tomato wedges.

Variation
Cook the cauliflower in boiling salted water until just tender, drain well and place on a hot serving dish. Top with crisply fried breadcrumbs and chopped hard-boiled egg and parsley.

Salade niçoise

Cooking time: 10 minutes
Preparation time: 10 minutes
Main cooking utensils: saucepan, salad bowl
Serves: 4–5

Imperial	Metric
1 lb. French beans	$\frac{1}{2}$ kg. French beans
8–12 oz. firm fresh tomatoes	200–300 g. firm fresh tomatoes
can anchovy fillets	can anchovy fillets
1 tablespoon oil	1 tablespoon oil
1 tablespoon vinegar and/or lemon juice	1 tablespoon vinegar and/or lemon juice
seasoning	seasoning
chopped parsley	chopped parsley
black olives	black olives

1. Cook the beans in boiling, salted water until just tender, drain and cool, then cut them into convenient lengths. Cutting them after cooking gives a firmer texture suitable for a salad.
2. Cut the tomatoes into quarters.
3. Cut the anchovy fillets into thinner strips or chop if wished.
4. Blend the oil from the can with the oil and vinegar and/or lemon juice and seasoning.
5. Toss the beans, tomatoes and anchovy fillets in the dressing and pile into the salad bowl. Top with chopped parsley and black olives.

Variation
Flaked canned tuna can be included in the ingredients, and quartered hard-boiled eggs added with the parsley and black olives at the end. The salad is then substantial enough to be served as a light luncheon dish.

Mixed salad platter

Cooking time: 10 minutes
Preparation time: 30 minutes
Main cooking utensils: saucepan, mixing bowl
Serves: 6–8

Imperial	Metric
8 oz. potatoes (preferably new)	200 g. potatoes (preferably new)
1 medium-sized can sweetcorn	1 medium-sized can sweetcorn
4 oz. cooked peas	100 g. cooked peas
$\frac{1}{4}$ pint mayonnaise	125 ml. mayonnaise
(see page 27)	(see page 27)
1 head celery	1 head celery
1 small cauliflower	1 small cauliflower
6–8 small tomatoes	6–8 small tomatoes
seasoning	seasoning
2 oz. grated Cheddar cheese	50 g. grated Cheddar cheese
1 cooked beetroot	1 cooked beetroot
oil and vinegar dressing	oil and vinegar dressing
(see page 31)	(see page 31)
1 onion	1 onion
8 oz. carrots	200 g. carrots
1 small cucumber	1 small cucumber
1 bunch watercress	1 bunch watercress
1 small red cabbage	1 small red cabbage

1. Scrub the potatoes and boil them in their jackets. Skin and dice and mix with the sweetcorn, peas and mayonnaise.
2. Wash the celery, cut into 3-inch (7-cm.) lengths and then cut these down almost to the base. Put these into iced water for one hour so that they open out in flowers.
3. Divide the cauliflower into sprigs, and cook these until barely tender, drain and cool. Scoop out the centre of the tomatoes, chop the pulp, season and mix it with the grated cheese. Pile this into the tomato cases and top with the cauliflower sprigs.
4. Cut the beetroot into large squares and toss in oil and vinegar. Top with thinly sliced onion rings.
5. Peel or scrape the carrots then grate them very coarsely. Season well.
6. Slice the cucumber thinly and mix with a little oil and vinegar dressing.
7. Wash and dry sprigs of watercress.
8. Discard the coarse outer leaves from the red cabbage, wash and put the cabbage to soak in cold water for a short time. Dry and shred very finely, and toss in oil and vinegar dressing.
9. Pile the potato salad into a bowl in the centre of the platter and arrange the red cabbage around this. Place the rest of the salad in piles around the dish and garnish with the watercress sprigs.

Stuffed celeriac or celery

Cooking time: 1 hour 5 minutes (see stage 3)
Preparation time: 20 minutes plus 20 minutes for roll to stand
Main cooking utensils: saucepan, ovenproof dish
Oven temperature: moderately hot (375°F., 190°C., Gas Mark 5)
Oven position: just above centre
Serves: 4

Imperial	Metric
2 medium celeriac or 4 heads celery	2 medium celeriac or 4 heads celery
squeeze lemon juice or few drops vinegar	squeeze lemon juice or few drops vinegar
seasoning	seasoning
Filling:	*Filling:*
6 oz. cooked meat	150 g. cooked meat
1 egg	1 egg
2 oz. butter	50 g. butter
1 small roll	1 small roll
6 tablespoons milk	6 tablespoons milk
pinch garlic seasoning	pinch garlic seasoning
pinch powdered nutmeg	pinch powdered nutmeg
pinch curry powder	pinch curry powder
1–2 apples	1–2 apples
½ pint thin cream	250 ml. thin cream
Garnish:	*Garnish:*
2 tomatoes	2 tomatoes
parsley sprigs	parsley sprigs

1. If using celeriac, peel, wash well and cut it in half. If using celery, cut away the base of the heads and wash well.

2. To keep celeriac roots white, add a few drops lemon juice or vinegar to the water in which the celeriac is washed, this is not necessary with celery.

3. Simmer in salted water until tender, again adding a little lemon juice or vinegar while cooking celeriac. Celery will be tender in about 20 minutes, but celeriac takes about 40 minutes.

4. Mince the meat, or chop very finely, blend with the egg, melted butter and the roll (soaked for 20 minutes in the milk then beaten until smooth), seasoning, nutmeg, curry powder and peeled, grated apple.

5. Stuff the celeriac or celery with this mixture, put into a greased dish, pour the cream round, season this, and bake for about 20 minutes. Serve topped with thick slices of tomato and sprigs of parsley.

Note: The cream becomes golden brown with cooking.

Transylvanian sauerkraut

Cooking time: 1 hour 20 minutes or 55 minutes (see stage 1)
Preparation time: 20 minutes
Main cooking utensils: large saucepan, ovenproof dish with lid or foil (see stage 3)
Oven temperature: moderately hot (375°F., 190°C., Gas Mark 5)
Oven position: just above centre
Serves: 4

Imperial	Metric
8–10 oz. sauerkraut or small cabbage	200–250 g. sauerkraut or small cabbage
seasoning	seasoning
2 onions	2 onions
1 oz. lard or surplus fat from meats	25 g. lard or surplus fat from meats
$\frac{1}{4}$ pint sour cream or thin cream and 2 teaspoons lemon juice	125 ml. sour cream or thin cream and 2 teaspoons lemon juice
4 small pork chops	4 small pork chops
4 thick rashers bacon (those shown come from the back)	4 thick rashers bacon (those shown come from the back)
4 sausages	4 sausages

1. Rinse the sauerkraut in cold water, drain, cook for 30 minutes only in well-seasoned water. If using cabbage, shred finely and cook for about 5 minutes only until half-cooked; season well.
2. Peel and slice the onions, fry in hot lard (or fat removed from the pork or bacon) until just tender, blend with the sauerkraut or cabbage together with the sour cream.
3. Put into a shallow dish, top with the pork, cook for 25 minutes, add the bacon and sausages and continue cooking for a further 20–25 minutes. If the meat is to be crisp, do not cover the dish, but make sure the meat covers the sauerkraut to prevent it drying.
4. Serve hot with potatoes, noodles or rice.

Variation
Often about 3 oz. (75 g.) cooked rice is added to this dish, and the pre-cooked meat diced and packed in layers with the sauerkraut, so you have a layer of sauerkraut, then rice, then meat and so on.

Ragoût of tomatoes and peppers

Cooking time: 35 minutes
Preparation time: 15 minutes
Main cooking utensil: large saucepan
Serves: 5

Imperial	**Metric**
5 green peppers	5 green peppers
seasoning	seasoning
1½–2 lb. ripe tomatoes	¾–1 kg. ripe tomatoes
1 red pepper (capsicum)	1 red pepper (capsicum)
1–2 cloves garlic (optional) and/or 1–2 medium-sized onions	1–2 cloves garlic (optional) and/or 1–2 medium-sized onions
2–3 tablespoons oil	2–3 tablespoons oil
¼ pint white wine	125 ml. white wine
1 teaspoon chopped fresh oregano (wild marjoram) or fresh marjoram or pinch dried marjoram	1 teaspoon chopped fresh oregano (wild marjoram) or fresh marjoram or pinch dried marjoram
1 oz. capers (see note)	25 g. capers (see note)

1. Cut a slice from each green pepper so that the inside core and seeds may be removed.
2. Simmer for about 5 minutes in boiling salted water, drain.
3. Skin the tomatoes if wished, and chop coarsely. Dice the red pepper finely.
4. Crush or chop the garlic and onions, fry in the hot oil with diced red pepper and green peppers, then add the wine, oregano, tomatoes and seasoning.
5. Simmer gently for about 35 minutes.
6. Top with capers and serve with bowls of grated cheese.

Note: Fresh capers are shown in the picture but bottled ones could be used.

Celery in creamed egg sauce

Cooking time: 55 minutes
Preparation time: 15 minutes plus time to stand (see stage 1)
Main cooking utensils: saucepan, ovenproof dish
Oven temperature: moderate to moderately hot (350–375°F.,
    180–190°C., Gas Mark 4–5)
Oven position: centre
Serves: 4 as a main dish or 8 as an hors d'oeuvre

Imperial	Metric
1 lb. celery or celeriac (celery root)	$\frac{1}{2}$ kg. celery or celeriac (celery root)
seasoning	seasoning
$\frac{1}{2}$ oz. butter	15 g. butter
3 eggs	3 eggs
good pinch black pepper	good pinch black pepper
1 teaspoon paprika pepper	1 teaspoon paprika pepper
good pinch grated or powdered nutmeg	good pinch grated or powdered nutmeg
$\frac{1}{2}$ pint evaporated milk or thin cream	250 ml. evaporated milk or thin cream
Garnish:	*Garnish:*
chopped parsley	chopped parsley

1. Scrape and wash celery, cut into portions, peel and slice celeriac.
2. Cook the vegetable in well-seasoned water.
3. When tender, drain and put into a buttered dish.
4. Beat the eggs with the remaining ingredients.
5. Pour over the vegetable, bake for approximately 30 minutes, garnish with parsley.

Note: If using celeriac, add 1 tablespoon vinegar or lemon juice to the cooking water at stage 2; this helps keep it white.

Variation
Use broccoli or asparagus.

Asparagus with hard-boiled eggs

Cooking time: 20–25 minutes
Preparation time: 15 minutes
Main cooking utensils: 2 saucepans
Serves: 4

Imperial	Metric
1 good-sized bundle of asparagus	1 good-sized bundle of asparagus
seasoning	seasoning
3 eggs	3 eggs
parsley	parsley
radishes	radishes
Dressing:	*Dressing:*
good pinch salt	good pinch salt
pepper	pepper
sugar	sugar
mustard	mustard
1 tablespoon lemon juice	1 tablespoon lemon juice
1 tablespoon tarragon vinegar	1 tablespoon tarragon vinegar
4 tablespoons olive oil	4 tablespoons olive oil

1. Cut the base from the asparagus, then scrape the remaining white part of the stalks to clean.

2. Wash well in cold water, taking care not to break the tips.

3. Drain well, then tie into 3—4 bundles. It is better to cook the asparagus in smaller bundles to make sure of even cooking; in one large bundle the outer stalks tend to be cooked before the inner ones.

4. Stand upright in a pan of well seasoned water and cook steadily. If the water boils too rapidly the asparagus tends to fall over.

5. Test to see if it is cooked by pressing the stalks; they should feel very tender. Drain carefully and season.

6. Meanwhile, boil the eggs for 10 minutes to hard-boil, shell, chop the yolks and whites separately, chop the parsley, slice the radishes.

7. Blend together the ingredients for the dressing, coat the asparagus with this. Garnish it with lines of egg yolk, egg white, parsley and radishes.

Variation

To serve as a hot hors d'oeuvre, toss in hot butter.

Fennel with paprika pepper sauce

Cooking time: 25 minutes
Preparation time: 15 minutes plus time for fennel to soak
Main cooking utensils: 2 saucepans, grill pan or frying pan
Serves: 6

Imperial	Metric
6 roots of sweet fennel (see note)	6 roots of sweet fennel (see note)
seasoning	seasoning
Sauce:	*Sauce:*
2 oz. butter	50 g. butter
1 clove garlic (optional)	1 clove garlic (optional)
1½ oz. flour	40 g. flour
½ pint milk	250 ml. milk
¼ pint thin cream	125 ml. thin cream
2—3 teaspoons paprika pepper	2—3 teaspoons paprika pepper
½—1 tablespoon tomato purée	½—1 tablespoon tomato purée
Garnish:	*Garnish:*
cooked bacon or chopped ham	cooked bacon or chopped ham
chopped parsley	chopped parsley

1. Pull off any damaged layers on the outside of the fennel roots, put to soak in cold water for an hour if possible, this makes the roots very firm and crisp.

2. Put into boiling, salted water, cook until just tender.

3. Meanwhile make the sauce. Heat butter, stir in the crushed garlic and flour, add the milk, cook until thick and smooth.

4. Stir in the cream, blended with paprika, cook for several minutes.

5. Remove the pan from the heat, add the tomato purée, do not re-boil the sauce.

6. Dice the grilled or fried bacon or ham.

7. Pour the sauce over the well-drained fennel, garnish with bacon or ham and parsley.

Note: These are 2 kinds of fennel, one is a herb with feathery leaves, the other, as in the picture, is a thick root. Add the chopped herb or leaves to sauces served with fish. If the fennel is purchased with leaves, remove these and use in salads and sauces.

Variation

Serve chopped fennel raw or cooked in salads, toss in oil or vinegar. Blend chopped anchovy fillets into cottage cheese, add chopped olives, and stuff the stems with this.

Mushroom mould

Cooking time: 45 minutes
Preparation time: 35 minutes
Main cooking utensils: saucepan, frying pan, 2- to 3-pint
  (1- to 1½-litre) mould
Oven temperature: moderately hot (400°F., 200°C., Gas Mark 6)
Oven position: centre
Serves: 6

Imperial	Metric
2 lb. old potatoes, weight before peeling	1 kg. old potatoes, weight before peeling
seasoning	seasoning
5 oz. butter	125 g. butter
2–3 oz. cheese, Gruyère, Cheddar or Parmesan	50–75 g. cheese, Gruyère, Cheddar or Parmesan
3 tablespoons thick cream	3 tablespoons thick cream
1 tablespoon chopped parsley	1 tablespoon chopped parsley
1 clove garlic (optional)	1 clove garlic (optional)
2 medium-sized onions	2 medium-sized onions
8 oz. mushrooms	200 g. mushrooms
4 tablespoons concentrated tomato purée	4 tablespoons concentrated tomato purée
good pinch sugar (optional)	good pinch sugar (optional)
Garnish:	*Garnish:*
celery leaves or parsley	celery leaves or parsley

1. Peel and cook the potatoes steadily in boiling, salted water, do not allow them to cook too quickly or they become watery, drain, sieve or mash well until very smooth.

2. Add 2 oz. (50 g.) butter, the grated cheese and cream to the potatoes together with the parsley; season the mixture well.

3. Heat the remaining butter, fry the finely chopped garlic and onions, remove from the pan and fry the mushrooms in the butter remaining in the pan.

4. Blend the onion and garlic with the tomato purée, add a pinch sugar to give a slightly sweet flavour.

5. Put half the tomato purée into the greased mould, then one third of the potato, the remaining tomato mixture, more potato, then half the fried mushrooms.

6. Cover with the remaining potato mixture (keep the remaining mushrooms hot).

7. Bake for approximately 20 minutes and turn out. Top and garnish with mushrooms and celery leaves or parsley.

Fried courgettes

Cooking time: few minutes
Preparation time: 10 minutes plus time to stand
Main cooking utensil: frying pan
Serves: 4

Imperial	Metric
8–12 courgettes	8–12 courgettes
seasoning	seasoning
½ oz. flour	15 g. flour
12 tablespoons olive oil	12 tablespoons olive oil
2 oz. butter	50 g. butter
6 oz. cooked ham	150 g. cooked ham
Garnish:	*Garnish:*
1–2 oz. Parmesan cheese, grated	25–50 g. Parmesan cheese, grated
2–3 teaspoons freshly chopped parsley and sweet basil	2–3 teaspoons freshly chopped parsley and sweet basil

1. Wash and dice the courgettes, sprinkle with a little salt and leave to stand for 30 minutes, this removes some of the bitter taste.

2. Drain off any liquid and coat the courgettes in the seasoned flour.

3. Heat the oil and butter in a pan and toss the courgette cubes in this, add the chopped ham when the courgettes are nearly tender.

4. Sprinkle with the cheese and chopped herbs just before serving.

Variation

Coat the sliced courgettes thickly in 1½ oz. (40 g.) flour and fry them in deep hot oil until crisp and golden brown on the outside. Drain on absorbent paper, pour a little white wine, vinegar or lemon juice over them and top with chopped parsley and a little chopped oregano.

Mushroom fondue

Cooking time: 14–20 minutes
Preparation time: 20 minutes
Main cooking utensils: saucepan, frying pan, grill
Serves: 6–8

Imperial	Metric
1 lb. mushrooms	$\frac{1}{2}$ kg. mushrooms
1 onion	1 onion
4 oz. luxury margarine	100 g. luxury margarine
1 oz. flour	25 g. flour
$\frac{1}{4}$ pint milk	125 ml. milk
$\frac{1}{2}$ pint thin cream	250 ml. thin cream
seasoning	seasoning
1 tablespoon chopped parsley	1 tablespoon chopped parsley
4 oz. Cheddar cheese, grated	100 g. Cheddar cheese, grated
For dipping:	*For dipping:*
$\frac{1}{2}$ large white loaf (unsliced)	$\frac{1}{2}$ large white loaf (unsliced)
2 teaspoons curry powder	2 teaspoons curry powder
6 rashers streaky bacon	6 rashers streaky bacon
4 oz. Cheddar cheese, cut in 24 thin pieces	100 g. Cheddar cheese, cut in 24 thin pieces
celery sticks	celery sticks
carrot sticks	carrot sticks

1. Wash, but do not peel the mushrooms, just trim the ends of the stalks, slice thinly.

2. Chop the peeled onion finely.

3. Heat 2 oz. (50 g.) margarine and fry the mushrooms and onion for 5 minutes, stirring once or twice.

4. Blend in the flour and cook gently for 2–3 minutes.

5. Gradually add the milk and cream, bring to the boil and cook until thickened, season.

6. Add the parsley and cheese. Do not boil again.

7. Remove the crusts from the bread and cut into $\frac{3}{4}$-inch ($1\frac{1}{2}$-cm.) cubes. Heat the remaining margarine with the curry powder, fry the bread until golden. Drain well.

8. Remove the rinds from the bacon and quarter the rashers, wrap round fingers of cheese, secure with wooden cocktail sticks. Grill for several minutes.

9. Serve immediately with the bread cubes, bacon rolls, celery and carrot sticks. Makes a complete light meal.

Mushroom and cheese escalopes

Cooking time: 15–20 minutes
Preparation time: 15 minutes
Main cooking utensils: 2 frying pans
Serves: 4

Imperial	Metric
2 oz. Camembert cheese	50 g. Camembert cheese
2 oz. soft breadcrumbs	50 g. soft breadcrumbs
1 oz. butter	25 g. butter
seasoning	seasoning
good pinch mixed herbs	good pinch mixed herbs
1 small can mushrooms	1 small can mushrooms
4 very thin slices veal	4 very thin slices veal
Coating:	*Coating:*
1 egg	1 egg
2 oz. soft breadcrumbs	50 g. soft breadcrumbs
To fry:	*To fry:*
3 oz. butter	75 g. butter
Garnish:	*Garnish:*
2 oz. butter	50 g. butter
few drops anchovy essence or tomato ketchup	few drops anchovy essence or tomato ketchup
1 oz. Camembert cheese and a few mushrooms (see stage 1)	25 g. Camembert cheese and a few mushrooms (see stage 1)
1 tablespoon chopped parsley	1 tablespoon chopped parsley
4 tomatoes	4 tomatoes
2 lemons	2 lemons
parsley sprigs	parsley sprigs

1. Mash the cheese, mix with the crumbs, softened butter, seasoning, herbs, and three-quarters of the drained, chopped mushrooms. The remaining mushrooms will be used for the garnish.

2. Spread the mixture over half of each slice of meat, then fold the meat to make a sandwich, secure with one or two wooden cocktail sticks while coating.

3. Brush each side of the meat with beaten egg and coat in crumbs.

4. Fry steadily in the hot butter until tender.

5. Meanwhile blend the butter with either the anchovy essence or the ketchup, mushrooms and cheese, and the parsley.

6. Form into pats and chill.

7. Skin and chop half the tomatoes, season and cook for a few minutes.

8. Slice the remaining tomatoes and one lemon, halve and 'van-dyke' the second lemon.

9. Serve very hot with the garnishes.

Asparagus and other vegetable omelettes

Cooking time: 35 minutes or 20 minutes with canned asparagus
Preparation time: 20 minutes
Main cooking utensils: 2 saucepans, omelette pan
Serves: 4

Imperial	Metric
1 bundle asparagus or medium can asparagus	1 bundle asparagus or medium can asparagus
seasoning	seasoning
Sauce:	*Sauce:*
1 oz. butter	25 g. butter
1 oz. flour	25 g. flour
12 tablespoons milk	12 tablespoons milk
3 tablespoons asparagus stock or liquid from can	3 tablespoons asparagus stock or liquid from can
seasoning	seasoning
Omelettes:	*Omelettes:*
5–6 eggs, separated	5–6 eggs, separated
2 oz. flour	50 g. flour
¼ pint milk	125 ml. milk
seasoning	seasoning
little grated nutmeg	little grated nutmeg
1 medium onion	1 medium onion
3 oz. butter	75 g. butter
2 tablespoons oil	2 tablespoons oil
2 oz. grated Fontina, Gruyère or Parmesan cheese	50 g. grated Fontina, Gruyère or Parmesan cheese
1 tomato	1 tomato

1. Prepare and cook the asparagus, or heat the canned asparagus, season.
2. Make a sauce with the butter, flour, milk and asparagus stock, season.
3. For the omelettes, blend the beaten egg yolks, flour, milk, seasoning and grated nutmeg together.
4. Fry the chopped onion in 1 oz. (25 g.) butter, when tender add to the omelette mixture.
5. Blend the asparagus with the sauce made at stage 2, keep hot, reserve a little asparagus for garnish.
6. Whisk the egg whites until stiff, fold into the omelette mixture.
7. Heat the butter and oil in a pan, put in a quarter of the omelette mixture, fry until lightly set on the bottom. Remove from the pan. Repeat with the remaining mixture to give 4 omelettes.
8. Fold the omelettes round the asparagus and sauce, sprinkle lightly with cheese, add thin strips of tomato and brown under a hot grill for 2–3 minutes.
9. Garnish with asparagus tips.

Note: To keep omelettes hot during preparation, put on an uncovered dish in a low oven.

Onion and tomato yeast dough

Cooking time: 1 hour
Preparation time: 40 minutes plus time for dough
Main cooking utensils: saucepan, baking tin or tray
Oven temperature: hot (425–450°F., 220–230°C., Gas Mark 7–8)
Oven position: centre
Serves: 6 as an appetiser or 12 as a light meal

Imperial	Metric
Dough:	*Dough:*
$\frac{1}{2}$ oz. yeast or 2 teaspoons dried yeast and 1 teaspoon sugar (see stage 1)	15 g. yeast or 2 teaspoons dried yeast and 1 teaspoon sugar (see stage 1)
$\frac{1}{2}$ pint water	250 ml. water
1 lb. flour, preferably plain	400 g. flour, preferably plain
seasoning	seasoning
1 tablespoon oil	1 tablespoon oil
Topping:	*Topping:*
3 tablespoons oil	3 tablespoons oil
1$\frac{1}{2}$ lb. onions	$\frac{3}{4}$ kg. onions
1 lb. tomatoes	$\frac{1}{2}$ kg. tomatoes
1–2 cans anchovy fillets	1–2 cans anchovy fillets
about 18 black olives	about 18 black olives

1. Dissolve the yeast in tepid water. If using dried yeast, sprinkle it on to tepid water to which one teaspoon of sugar has been added.

2. Sieve the flour with plenty of seasoning, add the oil and yeast liquid, knead well.

3. Cover the dough with a cloth or polythene bag and allow to prove in a warm place for about 1$\frac{1}{2}$–2 hours, until double in bulk.

4. Meanwhile heat the oil for the topping and cook the onions very slowly until really soft, adding the skinned, sliced tomatoes towards the end of the cooking time, season.

5. Knead the risen dough, form either into a round or oblong on a greased, warmed tin.

6. Cover the top of the dough with the onion and tomato mixture, anchovy fillets and olives.

7. Allow to prove again for approximately 20 minutes (this step could be omitted if in a hurry).

8. Bake for 20 minutes until the dough is firm. Serve hot or cold as an appetiser or light meal.

Variation

Omit tomatoes and increase onions to 2 lb. (1 kg.).

Cheese vegetable pie

Cooking time: 50 minutes
Preparation time: 30 minutes
Main cooking utensil: 8-inch (20-cm.) pie plate or similar dish
Oven temperature: moderately hot to hot (400–425°F., 200–220°C.,
  Gas Mark 6–7)
Oven position: just above centre
Serves: 4

Imperial	Metric
6 oz. flour	150 g. flour
pinch salt	pinch salt
shake pepper	shake pepper
cayenne pepper and dry mustard	cayenne pepper and dry mustard
2½ oz. butter or fat	65 g. butter or fat
3 oz. Cheddar cheese, finely grated	75 g. Cheddar cheese, finely grated
1 egg yolk	1 egg yolk
water	water
Filling:	*Filling:*
1 lb. mixed vegetables (carrots, turnips, beans, peas, sprigged cauliflower or any one of these)	½ kg. mixed vegetables (carrots, turnips, beans, peas, sprigged cauliflower or any one of these)
seasoning	seasoning
1 oz. butter	25 g. butter
1 oz. flour	25 g. flour
¼ pint milk	125 ml. milk
4 oz. grated cheese	100 g. grated cheese
Glaze:	*Glaze:*
1 egg white	1 egg white

1. Sieve the flour and seasonings, rub in the fat, add the grated cheese and bind with the egg yolk and water.
2. While preparing the vegetables, stand the pastry in a cool place to make it easier to handle.
3. Dice the vegetables where necessary, cook until almost tender in boiling, salted water, strain and retain ¼ pint (125 ml.) of the liquid.
4. Heat the butter in the vegetable pan, stir in the flour, cook for several minutes then gradually blend in the milk and vegetable stock.
5. Boil until thickened, season well after tasting and add the cheese, do not cook again once the cheese is added.
6. Mix the vegetables with the sauce, put the mixture into a shallow pie plate or dish and cool if necessary.
7. Top with the pastry, using the trimmings to make leaves for decoration. Brush with egg white, cook until the pastry is golden brown and firm. Serve hot.

Caesar hotpot

Cooking time: 15 minutes
Preparation time: 15 minutes
Main cooking utensils: saucepan, frying pan
Serves: 4

Imperial	Metric
1 lb. young carrots	400 g. young carrots
8 oz. fresh peas	200 g. fresh peas
8 oz. diced new potatoes	200 g. diced new potatoes
or very small potatoes	or very small potatoes
seasoning	seasoning
Dressing:	*Dressing:*
seasoning	seasoning
1 teaspoon made mustard	1 teaspoon made mustard
2 tablespoons vinegar	2 tablespoons vinegar
4 tablespoons oil	4 tablespoons oil
Croûtons:	*Croûtons:*
2 slices bread	2 slices bread
2 oz. butter or fat	50 g. butter or fat
6 oz. white Cheddar or	150 g. white Cheddar or
Gruyère cheese	Gruyère cheese
Garnish:	*Garnish:*
olives	olives

1. Scrape the carrots and dice neatly.
2. Cook these with the peas and new potatoes in boiling, salted water until just tender.
3. Drain very well.
4. For the dressing, blend the seasoning with the vinegar and oil and toss the hot vegetables in this, they absorb the flavour better when warm.
5. Dice the bread and fry in the hot butter or fat until crisp and golden brown.
6. Dice the cheese neatly.
7. Arrange the vegetables in a deep dish or a shallow dish on a bed of lettuce if preferred, and top with the croûtons of bread (these should be hot for they make a pleasing contrast to the cold vegetables and cheese).
8. Put the cheese and olives on the salad, turn and serve

Variation
Bacon hotpot: Dice 2 fairly thick rashers of bacon and fry until crisp; chop. Blend the vegetables with dressing, as above, mix with the croûtons and bacon, top with coarsely grated or diced cheese.

Courgette mould

Cooking time: 1¼ hours
Preparation time: 30 minutes
Main cooking utensils: saucepan, frying pan, 2-pint (1-litre) mould or basin, tin of water for mould
Oven temperature: moderate (325–350°F., 170–180°C., Gas Mark 3–4)
Oven position: centre
Serves: 6

Imperial	Metric
Sauce:	*Sauce:*
¾ pint milk	375 ml. milk
1 small onion	1 small onion
1 carrot	1 carrot
1 stick celery	1 stick celery
1½ oz. butter	40 g. butter
1½ oz. flour	40 g. flour
seasoning	seasoning
Mould:	*Mould:*
4–6 medium-sized courgettes	4–6 medium-sized courgettes
2 medium-sized onions	2 medium-sized onions
1½ oz. butter	40 g. butter
1½ tablespoons olive oil	1½ tablespoons olive oil
3 eggs	3 eggs
4 oz. Parmesan cheese, grated	100 g. Parmesan cheese, grated

1. Infuse the milk with the onion, carrot and celery for 15 minutes, i.e., heat for a few minutes, then stand in a warm place.
2. Melt the butter in a large pan, stir in flour and cook for several minutes. Add the strained milk and seasoning, cook until smooth and well-thickened.
3. Slice, but do not peel the courgettes and chop peeled onions finely, cook for about 10 minutes in butter and oil.
4. Put some of the slices of courgette aside for garnish, but blend the rest, and the onions with the sauce.
5. Beat in the eggs and grated cheese, and spoon the mixture into the mould or basin.
6. Cover with buttered paper or foil, stand in a dish of water and set for 1 hour in the oven.
7. Turn out and top with slices of courgette.

Variation
Add 1 tablespoon chopped parsley and ½ teaspoon chopped sage. Use Cheddar or Gruyère cheese.

Autumn vegetable pie

Cooking time: 35 minutes
Preparation time: 30 minutes plus time for pastry to stand
Main cooking utensil: 10-inch (25-cm.) pie plate
Oven temperature: hot to very hot (450–475°F., 230–240°C.,
    Gas Mark 8–9) then moderate to moderately hot (350–375°F.,
    180–190°C., Gas Mark 4–5)
Oven position: centre
Serves: 6–8

Imperial	Metric
Rough puff pastry:	*Rough puff pastry:*
8 oz. plain flour	200 g. plain flour
pinch salt	pinch salt
6 oz. lard	150 g. lard
water to mix	water to mix
Filling:	*Filling:*
12 oz. mushrooms	300 g. mushrooms
1 lb. tomatoes	400 g. tomatoes
1 lb. leeks	400 g. leeks
seasoning	seasoning
Glaze:	*Glaze:*
1 egg	1 egg
little water	little water
Garnish:	*Garnish:*
parsley	parsley

1. Sieve the flour and salt, cut in the lard, blend with water. Do not attempt to rub the lard in.

2. Roll out to an oblong shape, fold in three, seal the ends; 'rib', i.e., depress the pastry at regular intervals.

3. Turn at right angles, repeat the procedure to give five foldings and five rollings, put the pastry away between these in a cool place.

4. For the filling, wash and slice the mushrooms, do not peel them as the skin gives flavour.

5. Skin, quarter and remove the seeds from the tomatoes.

6. Wash the leeks well, use the white part only; the green tops can be used in soups and stews.

7. Arrange the vegetables in layers in the pie plate, season well.

8. Roll out the pastry, put a narrow strip round the edge of the plate, cover with a round of pastry, seal the edges and use egg beaten with water for the glaze.

9. Bake for 10–15 minutes, to brown and make the pastry rise, at the higher temperature, then lower the heat for a further 20–25 minutes. Garnish with parsley.

Vegetable savarin

Cooking time: 30 minutes
Preparation time: 25 minutes plus time for dough to prove
Main cooking utensils: baking tray, 2 saucepans
Oven temperature: hot (425–450°F., 220–230°C., Gas Mark 7–8)
Oven position: above centre
Serves: 6–8

Imperial	Metric
½ oz. yeast (poor weight) or 2 teaspoons dried yeast	15 g. yeast (poor weight) or 2 teaspoons dried yeast
1 teaspoon sugar	1 teaspoon sugar
6 tablespoons tepid milk	6 tablespoons tepid milk
8 oz. plain flour	200 g. plain flour
good pinch salt	good pinch salt
pepper and mustard	pepper and mustard
2 oz. butter	50 g. butter
2 oz. Parmesan cheese, finely grated	50 g. Parmesan cheese, finely grated
2 egg yolks	2 egg yolks
Glaze:	*Glaze:*
2 egg whites	2 egg whites
Filling:	*Filling:*
1 lb. mixed vegetables or large packet frozen mixed vegetables	½ kg. mixed vegetables or large packet frozen mixed vegetables
1 oz. butter	25 g. butter
Cheese sauce:	*Cheese sauce:*
2 oz. butter	50 g. butter
2 oz. flour	50 g. flour
1 pint milk	500 ml. milk
4 oz. Cheddar cheese, grated	100 g. Cheddar cheese, grated
seasoning	seasoning

1. Cream the fresh yeast with the sugar, add the tepid milk and a sprinkling of flour; if using dried yeast dissolve the sugar in tepid milk, add the dried yeast, stand for 10 minutes, add a sprinkling of flour, continue as with fresh yeast.

2. Sieve the remaining flour with the seasonings, rub in the butter, add the cheese, yeast liquid and egg yolks, knead until smooth.

3. Cover, allow to prove until double its original size, about 1 hour.

4. Knead until smooth, form into a round on a warmed baking tray.

5. Snip the dough at intervals, brush with egg white, prove for 15 minutes and bake in a hot oven until crisp and brown, about 30 minutes.

6. Meanwhile, cook the vegetables in salted water, drain and add the butter.

7. Make a sauce with the butter, flour and milk, when thickened add seasoning and the grated cheese. Heat only until the cheese melts.

8. Pile vegetables in the centre of the ring, serve the sauce separately.

Savoury cauliflower platter

Cooking time: 25 minutes
Preparation time: 20 minutes
Main cooking utensils: saucepan, frying pan, shallow ovenproof dish
Oven temperature: moderately hot (375°F., 190°C., Gas Mark 5)
Oven position: above centre
Serves: 4

Imperial	Metric
1 large cauliflower	1 large cauliflower
seasoning	seasoning
2 onions	2 onions
3 oz. butter	75 g. butter
1 teaspoon paprika	1 teaspoon paprika
1 teaspoon garlic seasoning	1 teaspoon garlic seasoning
1 red pepper and 2 tomatoes	1 red pepper and 2 tomatoes,
or 3 red peppers	or 3 red peppers
3 oz. soft breadcrumbs	75 g. soft breadcrumbs
4 oz. grated Gruyère cheese	100 g. grated Gruyère cheese
Garnish:	*Garnish:*
chopped parsley	chopped parsley

1. Divide the cauliflower into sprigs, cook in boiling, salted water until just tender, drain and return to the pan.
2. Meanwhile slice or chop the onions, fry in 2 oz. (50 g.) butter until very soft, add the paprika and garlic seasoning, add to the cauliflower and mix carefully together.
3. Put into the dish, top with the diced pepper and tomatoes, the pepper can be blanched for five minutes in boiling salted water if wished.
4. Cover with the crumbs, cheese and the rest of the butter, melted. Heat steadily under the grill or in the oven until golden. Serve at once garnished with parsley.

Variation
Cook the cauliflower as above. Make a sauce with 1 oz. (25 g.) butter, 1 oz. (25 g.) flour, $\frac{1}{4}$ pint (125 ml.) milk and $\frac{1}{4}$ pint (125 ml.) cauliflower stock. When smooth and thick stir in $\frac{1}{4}$ pint (125 ml.) thin cream. Season well. Cut 6 oz. (150 g.) Gruyère cheese into thin slices, put a thin layer of cheese into a dish, top with half the cauliflower and sauce, another layer of cheese, the remaining cauliflower and sauce, and a final layer of sliced cheese. Heat through in a moderately hot oven for 20–25 minutes.

Cheese and vegetable croquettes

Cooking time: 40 minutes
Preparation time: 25 minutes plus time for mixture to set
Main cooking utensils: 2 saucepans, frying pan
Serves: 5

Imperial	Metric
1 very small cauliflower	1 very small cauliflower
2 medium carrots	2 medium carrots
4 oz. peas or beans, weight when prepared	100 g. peas or beans, weight when prepared
seasoning	seasoning
Cheese sauce:	*Cheese sauce:*
2 oz. butter	50 g. butter
2 oz. flour	50 g. flour
¼ pint milk	125 ml. milk
¼ pint vegetable stock (see stage 2)	125 ml. vegetable stock (see stage 2)
½ teaspoon made mustard	½ teaspoon made mustard
6 oz. grated cheese, Cheddar or Gruyère	150 g. grated cheese, Cheddar or Gruyère
2 oz. white or brown bread-crumbs (optional, see stage 5)	50 g. white or brown bread-crumbs (optional, see stage 5)
Coating:	*Coating:*
1 oz. flour	25 g. flour
1–2 eggs	1–2 eggs
2–3 oz. coarse breadcrumbs	50–75 g. coarse breadcrumbs
To fry:	*To fry:*
3 oz. fat	75 g. fat

1. Divide the cauliflower into small sprigs, dice the carrots.
2. Cook the vegetables in well seasoned water until tender, do not overcook, strain and reserve ¼ pint (125 ml.) liquid.
3. Heat the butter, stir in the flour, cook for several minutes, add the milk and stock.
4. Bring to the boil, cook until thickened and season well. Add the mustard. Stir in the cheese and vegetables. Do not cook again once the cheese is added.
5. Allow the mixture to cool and become firm, there should be no need to add crumbs, but if a firmer texture is required they can be added.
6. Form into croquette shapes, sprinkle with seasoned flour, coat in beaten egg and crumbs. Fry in shallow fat until crisp. Drain on absorbent paper.
7. Make a tomato sauce; fry 1 chopped onion and 1 crushed clove garlic in the butter. Add 4 peeled, skinned and deseeded tomatoes, simmer until tender; add seasoning, a pinch of sugar and 1 tablespoon tomato purée.
8. Serve the croquettes with the sauce.

Bean and tomato hotpot

Cooking time: 3¼ hours
Preparation time: 15 minutes plus time for beans to soak
  overnight
Main cooking utensil: large saucepan
Serves: 4–5

Imperial	Metric
8 oz. butter beans	200 g. butter beans
seasoning	seasoning
about 1–1½ lb. neck of mutton or lamb	about ½–¾ kg. neck of mutton or lamb
2 large onions	2 large onions
1 clove garlic (optional)	1 clove garlic (optional)
2 oz. butter or fat	50 g. butter or fat
1–2 rashers bacon	1–2 rashers bacon
1 oz. flour	25 g. flour
¾–1 lb. tomatoes	300–400 g. tomatoes
sprinkling chopped rosemary or thyme, or pinch dried herbs	sprinkling chopped rosemary or thyme, or pinch dried herbs
¼ pint white wine (optional)	125 ml. white wine (optional)

1. Put the beans into a large container, cover with cold water, leave overnight. If preferred, soak in white stock for a richer flavour.

2. Put the beans, liquid and seasoning into a pan, simmer for 2 hours. Drain, save the liquid.

3. Cut the meat into convenient sized pieces.

4. Peel the onions, slice thickly, crush the garlic.

5. Heat the butter or fat, fry the onions and garlic, taking care they do not brown. Fry the finely chopped bacon.

6. Lift out of the pan; fry the meat, coated in seasoned flour, until well browned.

7. Lift this out of the pan, then return the beans, skinned sliced tomatoes, herbs, the onions, etc., to the pan, together with ¼ pint (125 ml.) bean liquid and white wine, or use ½ pint (250 ml.) bean liquid.

8. Add the meat, cover the pan tightly, simmer for 1 hour, add a little extra liquid from time to time if necessary. Serve with green salad or vegetable.

Note: Only a small amount of meat need be used, as beans provide protein as well as flavour.

Variation

Fry tiny sausages with the meat, remove and reheat at the end.

Potato croquettes

Cooking time: 35 minutes
Preparation time: 35 minutes
Main cooking utensils: saucepan, frying pan or saucepan and
   frying basket
Serves: 4–6

Imperial	Metric
1–1½ lb. old potatoes	½–¾ kg. pld potatoes
1–2 oz. margarine or butter	25–50 g. margarine or butter
seasoning	seasoning
little milk	little milk
Coating:	*Coating:*
1 tablespoon flour	1 tablespoon flour
seasoning	seasoning
1 egg	1 egg
1½–2 oz. crisp breadcrumbs	40–50 g. crisp breadcrumbs
To fry:	*To fry:*
shallow frying, 2–3 oz. fat or 3 tablespoons oil	shallow frying, 50–75 g. fat or 3 tablespoons oil
OR	OR
deep frying, 1¼–1½ lb. fat or 1¼–1½ pints oil	deep frying, generous ½–¾ kg. fat or approximately ¾ litre oil

1. Peel the potatoes, put them into boiling salted water, cook steadily until tender, then drain.

2. Mash, add the margarine, seasoning and a little milk — the mixture should be soft enough to form into finger shapes or rounds. Finger shapes are more suitable for shallow frying.

3. Coat in seasoned flour, then in beaten egg and crumbs.

4. Heat the fat in a frying pan or saucepan.

5. Heat until a cube of bread goes golden brown within 1 minute if using fat, or ½ minute if using oil. If the fat is too hot, the croquettes will break badly.

6. Put the croquettes into the hot fat or oil. If using a frying basket put this into the fat first, then put the croquettes into the fat gently.

7. Fry for a few minutes until crisp and golden brown, in shallow fat they will need turning.

8. Lift out and drain on crumpled tissue or absorbent paper. Serve with meat, poultry or fish.

Variation

Add grated cheese or a little chopped mixed herbs.

Potato dips

Cooking time: 20 minutes
Preparation time: 30 minutes
Main cooking utensils: saucepan, cocktail sticks
Makes: 24

Imperial	Metric
about 2 lb. tiny new potatoes	about 1 kg. tiny new potatoes
sprig mint	sprig mint
seasoning	seasoning
Spicy tomato dip:	*Spicy tomato dip:*
1 clove garlic, crushed, or	1 clove garlic, crushed, or
1 teaspoon grated onion	1 teaspoon grated onion
1 tablespoon oil	1 tablespoon oil
2 level teaspoons cornflour	2 level teaspoons cornflour
1 tablespoon lemon juice or	1 tablespoon lemon juice or
vinegar	vinegar
$\frac{3}{4}$ pint tomato juice	375 ml. tomato juice
2 teaspoons brown sugar	2 teaspoons brown sugar
little Worcestershire sauce	little Worcestershire sauce
seasoning	seasoning
Cheese dip:	*Cheese dip:*
6 oz. cream cheese	150 g. cream cheese
2 tablespoons cream	2 tablespoons cream
olives or spring onions	olives or spring onions
Tartare sauce:	*Tartare sauce:*
2 tablespoons chopped gherkins	2 tablespoons chopped gherkins
1 tablespoon chopped parsley	1 tablespoon chopped parsley
1 tablespoon chopped capers	1 tablespoon chopped capers
$\frac{1}{4}$ pint mayonnaise	125 ml. mayonnaise

1. Either scrape the potatoes and cook until tender with mint and seasoning, or cook and rub off the skin afterwards.
2. Put cocktail sticks in them and allow to cool – or serve hot if preferred.
3. Fry the garlic in the oil for a few minutes.
4. Blend the cornflour with the lemon juice and a little tomato juice.
5. Bring the rest of the tomato juice to the boil, add the cornflour mixture, sugar, sauce and seasoning, and cook until thickened. Pour into a bowl, allow to cool.
6. Blend the cream cheese with the cream, top with chopped olives or spring onions.
7. Add the gherkins, parsley and capers to the mayonnaise.
8. Arrange the bowls of dips round the potatoes.

Variation

Fry tiny potatoes or scoop out balls from a large potato with a scoop and fry these, drain well and serve hot.

Leeks in cheese sauce

Cooking time: 15 minutes plus time for cooking the leeks
Preparation time: 25 minutes
Main cooking utensils: saucepan, ovenproof dish
Oven temperature: hot (425–450°F., 220–230°C., Gas Mark 7–8)
Oven position: centre
Serves: 4–5

Imperial	Metric
8–12 good-sized leeks	8–12 good-sized leeks
Sauce:	*Sauce:*
1½ oz. butter	40 g. butter
1½ oz. flour	40 g. flour
½ pint leek stock (see stage 2)	250 ml. leek stock (see stage 2)
¼ pint milk	125 ml. milk
seasoning	seasoning
4–6 oz. grated cheese, Cheddar or Gruyère	100–150 g. grated cheese, Cheddar or Gruyère
2 oz. fat bacon	50 g. fat bacon

1. Prepare the leeks. Cut off the green tops a little above the white part (the green leaves can be used in soups or stews). Wash the leeks thoroughly under cold water. To ensure that no dirt is left between the leaves, put the leeks in really cold water for a time before cooking.

2. Put the leeks into a saucepan, just cover them with salted water and cook until barely tender; strain the stock and reserve ½ pint (250 ml.) for the sauce.

3. Melt the butter in the pan, add the flour and cook for a few minutes. Gradually stir in the stock and the milk. Cook until the sauce is thick and smooth. Season well, remove from the heat and stir in the cheese.

4. Put most of the sauce in a dish, top with the leeks, cover with remaining sauce and the bacon cut into thin strips.

5. Bake in a hot oven for 15 minutes.

Variation

Cold leeks can be served in a vinaigrette dressing. Cut the leeks into small pieces, cook in boiling salted water until just tender, drain well and while still hot blend with oil, vinegar, seasoning, a little chopped garlic and some skinned, chopped tomatoes. Serve very cold.

Cheese- and tomato-topped toasts

Cooking time: 5 minutes
Preparation time: 10 minutes
Main cooking utensil: grill pan
Serves: 4

Imperial	Metric
4 thick slices bread	4 thick slices bread
2 oz. butter	50 g. butter
4 oz. cheese, Mozzarella, Gruyère or Cheddar	100 g. cheese, Mozzarella, Gruyère or Cheddar
4 small tomatoes	4 small tomatoes
little oil or butter	little oil or butter
seasoning	seasoning
½ teaspoon oregano (wild marjoram)	½ teaspoon oregano (wild marjoram)
small can anchovy fillets	small can anchovy fillets
Garnish:	*Garnish:*
parsley or chervil	parsley or chervil
tomato wedges	tomato wedges

1. Toast the bread lightly on both sides.
2. Butter one side of the bread and cover with sliced cheese.
3. Top with the tomatoes, brushed with butter or oil and well seasoned, and a sprinkling of oregano.
4. Cook under the grill until the tomatoes have softened and the cheese has melted.
5. Top with rolls of anchovy fillets and garnish with parsley or chervil and tomato wedges.

Variation
Dip the slices of bread in well-seasoned milk and beaten egg, fry in hot oil or oil and butter until crisp and golden brown. Keep hot. Fry eggs in the hot fat and when nearly set, top with grated Parmesan cheese. Lift out carefully, put on to the hot fried bread and serve with raw tomatoes.

Mushrooms in wine

Cooking time: 20 minutes
Preparation time: 10 minutes
Main cooking utensil: saucepan
Serves: 5–6

Imperial	Metric
1½ lb. mushrooms	¾ kg. mushrooms
2 oz. butter	50 g. butter
2 tablespoons oil	2 tablespoons oil
juice and finely grated rind of	juice and finely grated rind of
1 large lemon	1 large lemon
½ pint white wine	275 ml. white wine
seasoning	seasoning
Garnish:	*Garnish:*
coarsely chopped parsley	coarsely chopped parsley

1. If the mushrooms are in good condition do not skin them as the skin contains much of the flavour. Wash the mushrooms well and trim the base of the stalks.

2. Heat the butter and oil in a large pan and toss the mushrooms in this taking care they do not brown or dry.

3. Add the lemon juice and rind, white wine and seasoning. Cook for about 20 minutes turning frequently to keep them moist. Leave the lid off the pan so that the liquid reduces and gives the mushrooms a good flavour.

4. Turn into a serving dish and top with coarsely chopped parsley. Serve with omelettes or other egg dishes.

Variation

Chopped onion and/or garlic can be fried in the butter and oil before adding the mushrooms. Small sausages can also be added. Fry these with the mushrooms, remove and add to the saucepan 10 minutes before serving.

Fried egg and vegetable stew

Cooking time: 35 minutes
Preparation time: 15 minutes
Main cooking utensils: saucepan, frying pan
Serves: 4–5

Imperial	Metric
4 good-sized firm tomatoes	4 good-sized firm tomatoes
1 aubergine	1 aubergine
2 green or 1 red and 1 green pepper	2 green or 1 red and 1 green pepper
1 medium-sized marrow or cucumber	1 medium-sized marrow or cucumber
2–3 tablespoons oil	2–3 tablespoons oil
1–2 cloves garlic	1–2 cloves garlic
2 large onions	2 large onions
seasoning	seasoning
chopped parsley	chopped parsley
8–10 eggs	8–10 eggs
fat or oil for frying	fat or oil for frying

1. Skin and chop the tomatoes; dice the aubergine leaving on the skin. Remove the cores and seeds from the peppers and cut the flesh into thin strips.
2. Peel and dice the marrow or cucumber.
3. Heat the oil in a pan. Crush the cloves of garlic and chop the onions finely. Fry until nearly tender in the oil.
4. Add all the vegetables, except the tomatoes, cover the pan tightly and cook slowly until the vegetables are just tender, about 35 minutes.
5. Add the tomatoes 15 minutes before the end of the cooking time, season well.
6. Pile the vegetables on to a hot serving plate, sprinkle with parsley and keep warm.
7. Fry the eggs in some fat or oil allowing one or two per person. Place them on the vegetables.

Variation
Courgettes instead of marrow or cucumber can be used, and 3 medium-sized new potatoes and 8 oz. (200 g.) chopped green beans can be substituted for the aubergine and peppers. The mixture should be cooked for 45 minutes until the vegetables are very tender.

Fish with onion sauce

Cooking time: 35–40 minutes
Preparation time: 25 minutes
Main cooking utensil: large pan
Serves: 4

Imperial	Metric
2 large or 4 smaller fish (grey (see note) or red mullet, trout, mackerel, codling and whiting are ideal)	2 large or 4 smaller fish (grey (see note) or red mullet, trout, mackerel, codling and whiting are ideal)
1 tablespoon chopped parsley	1 tablespoon chopped parsley
$\frac{1}{2}$ tablespoon chopped fennel	$\frac{1}{2}$ tablespoon chopped fennel
seasoning	seasoning
1 tablespoon olive oil	1 tablespoon olive oil
juice of 1 lemon	juice of 1 lemon
Sauce:	*Sauce:*
2 tablespoons olive oil	2 tablespoons olive oil
8 small onions or shallots	8 small onions or shallots
2 leeks	2 leeks
4 oz. mushrooms	100 g. mushrooms
$\frac{1}{2}$ pint dry white wine	250 ml. dry white wine
Garnish:	*Garnish:*
little chopped parsley	little chopped parsley
sprigs parsley or chervil	sprigs parsley or chervil

1. Clean the fish, sprinkle with the herbs, seasoning, oil and the lemon juice. Leave while preparing the sauce.
2. Heat the oil in the pan, fry the peeled onions or shallots and finely chopped leeks until nearly tender.
3. Add the thickly sliced mushrooms and wine, season lightly.
4. Simmer for 5 minutes.
5. Put in the fish; if too large for the pan, cut into neat pieces. Continue to cook without a lid on the pan so that the liquid evaporates.
6. Simmer until the fish is tender and there is about $\frac{1}{4}$ pint (125 ml.) liquid only. Top with the herbs.

Note: These must be cleaned with great care.

Variations
Omit the leeks, add 3–4 skinned, chopped tomatoes and 2–3 chopped anchovy fillets. Diced celery and blanched almonds could be added to the recipe at stage 4 together with strips of red and green pepper. The short cooking time keeps them firm in texture. Fennel root, cut in strips, may also be added.

Fish and mushroom cream

Cooking time: 30–40 minutes
Preparation time: 15 minutes plus time to stand if using dried mushrooms
Main cooking utensils: saucepan, frying pan
Serves: 5

Imperial	**Metric**
1–2 oz. dried mushrooms (see stage 1) or 2–4 oz. fresh mushrooms	25–50 g. dried mushrooms (see stage 1) or 50–100 g. fresh mushrooms
½ pint white stock	250 ml. white stock
5 small onions	5 small onions
seasoning	seasoning
5 rounds bread with crusts removed	5 rounds bread with crusts removed
¼ pint milk	125 ml. milk
1½ oz. flour	40 g. flour
3 oz. butter or 2–3 tablespoons oil	75 g. butter or 2–3 tablespoons oil
5 pieces cod or fresh haddock	5 pieces cod or fresh haddock
¼ pint white wine	125 ml. white wine
¼ pint thin cream or top of milk	125 ml. thin cream or top of milk
1 oz. grated Parmesan cheese	25 g. grated Parmesan cheese

1. The mushrooms shown in the picture are dried fungi (hence the uneven shape), often used in Italy. Soak for 1 hour in stock. (Fresh mushrooms can be used if dried ones are not obtainable, but the taste will be different.)

2. Put the stock (with the soaked mushrooms), onions and seasoning into the pan, simmer for 30–40 minutes or until the onions are tender. If using fresh mushrooms, add 5 minutes before the onions are cooked.

3. Dip the rounds of bread in the milk, do not let them become too soft. Dip in half the seasoned flour and fry in half the butter or oil until golden. Keep hot.

4. Coat the fish with the remaining well-seasoned flour, fry until golden brown and tender in the remaining butter or oil. Keep hot.

5. Blend the wine, cream and extra seasoning in the frying pan, cook gently until thickened. If too thick, add a little stock from the onion pan. Stir in the cheese.

6. Put the drained onions on to the fried bread, coat this layer with sauce, top with fish and mushrooms.

Fried cod with beans

Cooking time: 2 hours
Preparation time: 20 minutes plus overnight soaking of beans
Main cooking utensils: saucepan, frying pan
Serves: 4

Imperial	Metric
8 oz. red beans or ordinary white haricot beans (see note)	200 g. red beans or ordinary white haricot beans (see note)
about 2 pints white stock	about 1 litre white stock
$\frac{1}{4}$ pint red wine	125 ml. red wine
3 medium-sized shallots or onions	3 medium-sized shallots or onions
seasoning	seasoning
2 bay leaves	2 bay leaves
1 clove garlic (optional)	1 clove garlic (optional)
1 small red pepper	1 small red pepper
2 oz. butter	50 g. butter
2 tablespoons oil	2 tablespoons oil
8 small portions cod fillet	8 small portions cod fillet
$\frac{1}{2}$ oz. flour	15 g. flour
1 egg	1 egg
2 oz. crisp breadcrumbs	50 g. crisp breadcrumbs
Garnish:	*Garnish:*
chopped parsley	chopped parsley

1. Cover the beans with stock and soak them overnight, then simmer them gently until tender, adding the red wine, 1 finely chopped shallot or onion, seasoning to taste and the bay leaves.
2. When the beans are nearly tender, lift the lid off the saucepan, so the liquid evaporates.
3. Crush the garlic, dice the remaining shallots or onions and the red pepper (discarding the core and seeds), and fry steadily in the hot butter and oil until just soft; either lift out of the pan and keep hot, or push to one side of the pan.
4. Coat the portions of fish with seasoned flour, egg and crumbs. Fry until crisp and brown in the butter and oil, drain on absorbent paper and top with the fried vegetables and chopped parsley.
5. Serve the beans on a dish topped with the fish.

Note: Red beans or kidney beans should be soaked and cooked as ordinary white haricot beans, i.e., in water or white stock.

Gammon and asparagus rolls

Cooking time: 45 minutes if using fresh asparagus
Preparation time: 15 minutes
Main cooking utensils: saucepan, strainer, ovenproof dish
Oven temperature: moderately hot (375°F., 190°C., Gas Mark 5)
Oven position: above centre
Serves: 4

Imperial	Metric
8 oz. asparagus or 1 medium can asparagus	200 g. asparagus or 1 medium can asparagus
salt	salt
4 thin rashers gammon, rinds removed	4 thin rashers gammon, rinds removed
Sauce:	*Sauce:*
1 oz. butter	25 g. butter
1 oz. flour	25 g. flour
½ pint milk	250 ml. milk
4 tablespoons asparagus stock	4 tablespoons asparagus stock
4 oz. grated Cheddar cheese	100 g. grated Cheddar cheese
seasoning	seasoning
Garnish:	*Garnish:*
2 tomatoes	2 tomatoes
chopped parsley	chopped parsley

1. Cook the asparagus in boiling salted water until tender, or open the can of asparagus, drain carefully.

2. Wrap the thin gammon rashers round the asparagus, put into a dish and cook in the oven for 15 minutes.

3. Meanwhile make the cheese sauce. Melt the butter, stir in the flour and cook for several minutes.

4. Add the milk and asparagus stock, bring to the boil and cook until thickened.

5. Stir in the cheese and seasoning and pour the sauce over the asparagus.

6. Arrange halved tomatoes round the asparagus rolls, return to the oven to brown. Top with parsley. Serve hot with salad.

Variation

For a party: Prepare the rolls. Make the cheese sauce and pour over the rolls. Cover tightly to prevent the top drying and reheat in a moderately hot oven. Do not cook the sauce once the cheese has been added as this will make it tough with the extra heating in the oven.

Peas with bacon

Cooking time: 15–20 minutes
Preparation time: few minutes
Main cooking utensils: saucepan, frying pan
Serves: 4

Imperial	Metric
1 lb. fresh shelled or frozen peas	½ kg. fresh shelled or frozen peas
4 rashers bacon	4 rashers bacon
1 onion	1 onion
½–1 oz. butter or margarine	15–25 g. butter or margarine
seasoning	seasoning

1. Cook the shelled peas for 15–20 minutes, or the frozen peas as directed on the package.
2. Meanwhile, cook the bacon. Cut the bacon into narrow strips and fry until crisp; when nearly ready add the finely sliced onion and the butter and continue cooking until the onion is just tender, and separated into rings or pieces.
3. Drain the peas and season well, then add the bacon and onion.
4. Heat the peas and bacon together for a minute. Serve with a meat or vegetable dish.

Variation

Peas à la française: Arrange a layer of lettuce leaves – the outer ones will do – in a casserole or saucepan Add 1 lb. (½ kg.) fresh shelled peas, a few spring onions, 1 oz. (25 g.) butter and seasoning and cover with a second layer of lettuce leaves (the lettuce leaves must be wet). Cook slowly for 30–45 minutes on top of the cooker or in a moderate oven (375°F., 190°C., Gas Mark 5) in a covered casserole until the peas are tender. Serve with or without the lettuce.

Stew of bacon and vegetables

Cooking time: 35 minutes
Preparation time: 25 minutes
Main cooking utensil: large saucepan
Serves: 4

Imperial	Metric
about 12 oz. gammon or back bacon, cut in thick rashers	about 300 g. gammon or back bacon, cut in thick rashers
2 oz. butter	50 g. butter
8 oz. onions	200 g. onions
seasoning	seasoning
1½ lb. peas, weight before shelling, or equivalent in frozen peas (see stages 5 and 6)	¾ kg. peas, weight before shelling, or equivalent in frozen peas (see stages 5 and 6)
12 oz. new carrots, scraped	300 g. new carrots, scraped

1. Remove the bacon rinds and put them into the pan with the bacon. Cut the bacon into fingers.
2. Fry steadily until golden coloured, lift out, put on a plate, then add the butter to the pan.
3. Peel and slice the onions, toss in the butter until translucent, do not allow to brown.
4. If a great deal of fat remains, some could be spooned out, but a little fat is a good thing as it adds flavour to the vegetables; leave the bacon rinds in the pan.
5. Add approximately ½ pint (250 ml.) water and seasoning (be sparing with the salt); put in the fresh shelled peas and sliced carrots. Cook steadily for about 15–20 minutes, covering the pan tightly. If using frozen peas, cook the carrots for 15–20 minutes and add the peas with the bacon at stage 6.
6. Replace the bacon and continue cooking until the vegetables are quite soft. Remove the bacon rinds.
7. The liquid should have evaporated by the time the vegetables are cooked; if necessary remove the lid to increase evaporation.

Variation

Blend a little thin cream into the cooked vegetables and bacon. Soaked dried peas could be used, in which case increase the cooking time and the amount of liquid.

Ragoût of sausages and onions

Cooking time: 20 minutes
Preparation time: 10 minutes
Main cooking utensil: sauté or frying pan
Serves: 4–5

Imperial	Metric
2 oz. butter or fat	50 g. butter or fat
4–5 large onions	4–5 large onions
1½ lb. sausages	¾ kg. sausages
⅓ pint cheap white wine	175 ml. cheap white wine
seasoning	seasoning
pinch oregano (wild marjoram)	pinch oregano (wild marjoram)
or generous amount	or generous amount
chopped parsley	chopped parsley

1. Heat the butter or fat in the pan. Slice the onions thickly and fry them in the hot fat until they begin to turn golden brown. Remove from the pan.

2. Add the sausages to the pan, whole or divided into pieces. Fry them until they are golden brown on the outside and nearly cooked.

3. Return the onions and add the white wine. Season well and add the oregano or chopped parsley. Continue cooking for a further 10 minutes, then pile the mixture on to a hot serving dish.

Variation

Instead of white wine add ½ pint (250 ml.) beer blended with 1 tablespoon of flour or potato flour. Stir this into the mixture and continue cooking for a further 10 minutes, stirring occasionally. Serve with potatoes, carrots or other vegetables.

Potato and corned beef hash

Cooking time: 1¼–1½ hours
Preparation time: 15 minutes
Main cooking utensils: baking tray, frying pan
Oven temperature: moderately hot (375°F., 190°C., Gas Mark 5)
Oven position: centre
Serves: 4

Imperial	Metric
4 medium-sized potatoes or 2 really large ones	4 medium-sized potatoes or 2 really large ones
$\frac{1}{2}$–1 oz. butter or margarine	15—25 g. butter or margarine
2 oz. shortening or fat	50 g. shortening or fat
2 onions or equivalent in spring onions	2 onions or equivalent in spring onions
3–4 oz. streaky bacon	75—100 g. streaky bacon
12 oz. corned beef	300 g. corned beef
2 dessert apples	2 dessert apples
seasoning	seasoning
Topping:	*Topping:*
knob butter	knob butter
parsley	parsley

1. Wash and dry the potatoes, prick them to prevent the skins breaking, brush the skins with butter or margarine.
2. Put on a baking sheet and bake until soft, approximately $1\frac{1}{4}$–$1\frac{1}{2}$ hours in a moderately hot oven.
3. Split the potatoes through the centre and scoop out the centre pulp, trying to keep this in reasonable-sized pieces rather than allowing it to become soft and mashed.
4. Heat the shortening or fat in a pan and fry the chopped onions until nearly soft. Remove from the heat and add the finely chopped bacon, flaked corned beef, pieces of potato and diced apple (leave the peel on for extra flavour and colour). Season lightly.
5. Season the potato cases, pile the mixture back into them and return to the oven for about 10 minutes to heat through.
6. Serve topped with a knob of butter and a little chopped parsley; this is excellent for supper or as a main dish with a green vegetable.

Variation

Add 2—3 skinned, chopped tomatoes. Flavour with 1 teaspoon curry powder.

Bacon-stuffed peppers

Cooking time: 40 minutes
Preparation time: 20 minutes
Main cooking utensils: frying pan, saucepan, ovenproof dish, metal
 skewers
Oven temperature: moderately hot (400°F., 200°C., Gas Mark 6)
Oven position: centre
Serves: 4

Imperial	Metric
4 green or red peppers	4 green or red peppers
1 oz. margarine	25 g. margarine
Stuffing:	*Stuffing:*
8 oz. streaky or back bacon	200 g. streaky or back bacon
2 oz. margarine	50 g. margarine
1 medium-sized onion	1 medium-sized onion
3 oz. soft breadcrumbs or cooked rice	75 g. soft breadcrumbs or cooked rice
seasoning	seasoning
$\frac{1}{2}$ teaspoon powdered sage	$\frac{1}{2}$ teaspoon powdered sage
2 oz. mushrooms, chopped	50 g. mushrooms, chopped
Garnish:	*Garnish:*
4 rashers streaky or back bacon	4 rashers streaky or back bacon
parsley	parsley

1. Dice the bacon for the stuffing finely and fry in a pan.
2. Add the margarine and finely chopped onion, and continue frying until the bacon is very crisp and the onion soft.
3. Add the rest of the ingredients for the stuffing.
4. While the bacon is cooking, prepare the peppers.
5. Cut a slice from the top, remove the core and seeds, and cook the peppers for 5 minutes in boiling salted water. Drain carefully.
6. Pack the stuffing into the peppers and brush with the melted margarine. Bake in the oven for approximately 25 minutes.
7. While the peppers are cooking, cut the rashers of bacon into small pieces, roll and put on skewers. Put into the dish with the peppers to cook.
8. Remove the bacon rolls from the skewers and place on top of the peppers. Garnish with parsley and serve with baked tomatoes.

Variation
Use tomatoes in place of mushrooms in the stuffing.

Bean and meat casserole

Cooking time: 2¼ hours
Preparation time: 30 minutes plus overnight soaking for beans
Main cooking utensils: strong saucepan, deep casserole
Oven temperature: moderate (325–350°F., 170–180°C., Gas Mark 3–4)
Oven position: centre
Serves: 8

Imperial	**Metric**
2 lb. haricot beans	1 kg. haricot beans
6-oz. piece salt pork	150-g. piece salt pork
8 oz. lamb or mutton	200 g. lamb or mutton
1 small garlic sausage	1 small garlic sausage
3 oz. lard	75 g. lard
1 onion	1 onion
3–4 cloves	3–4 cloves
1 clove garlic or 1 teaspoon garlic salt	1 clove garlic or 1 teaspoon garlic salt
2 sprigs parsley	2 sprigs parsley
2 tablespoons concentrated tomato purée	2 tablespoons concentrated tomato purée
seasoning	seasoning
8 oz. tomatoes	200 g. tomatoes
3 oz. breadcrumbs	75 g. breadcrumbs
2 oz. butter	50 g. butter

1. Soak the haricot beans overnight. Drain.

2. Dice the meats and sausage and fry in the lard until evenly browned.

3. Place the beans, meats, onion stuck with cloves, crushed garlic or garlic salt, parsley, tomato purée and seasoning in a deep casserole.

4. Just cover with water and cook steadily for approximately 2 hours in a moderate oven.

5. Add the quartered tomatoes. Fry the breadcrumbs in butter and sprinkle on top.

6. Bake for a further few minutes. Serve with a green vegetable.

Mixed meats and vegetables on skewers

Cooking time: 10 minutes
Preparation time: 10 minutes
Main cooking utensils: 6 strong metal skewers, grill pan
Serves: 6

Imperial	Metric
4 oz. beef fillet	100 g. beef fillet
4 oz. veal fillet	100 g. veal fillet
4 oz. pork fillet	100 g. pork fillet
1 pig's kidney or 2–3 lambs' kidneys	1 pig's kidney or 2–3 lambs' kidneys
4 oz. lamb's or calf's liver	100 g. lamb's or calf's liver
1 teaspoon hot paprika · (see note)	1 teaspoon hot paprika (see note)
1 teaspoon curry powder	1 teaspoon curry powder
salt	salt
2–3 large onions	2–3 large onions
2–3 rashers lean bacon	2–3 rashers lean bacon
1–2 oz. butter	25–50 g. butter
1 tablespoon concentrated tomato purée	1 tablespoon concentrated tomato purée
2 tablespoons stock	2 tablespoons stock
6–8 oz. rice	150–200 g. rice
Garnish:	*Garnish:*
lettuce	lettuce
2 tomatoes	2 tomatoes
parsley	parsley

1. Cut the meats into neat pieces.
2. Sprinkle with the paprika, curry powder and a little salt.
3. Skin the onions and cut into rings; they will be fairly firm and crisp cooked this way, so if a softer onion ring is required, simmer the whole onions for a short time in salted water, dry well then cut into rings.
4. Divide the bacon into neat pieces, or form into rolls if preferred.
5. Thread all the meats and onions on to the skewers.
6. Blend the butter with the purée, stock and a little extra seasoning. Brush this over the skewers.
7. Cook under a hot grill, turning once or twice, until the food is cooked and tender.
8. Meanwhile cook the rice and arrange on hot plates. Top with the skewers and garnishes. Serve with tomato sauce.

Note: This spice is obtainable in most delicatessens.

Variation
Cheaper cuts of meat could be used, if marinated in a mixture of oil and lemon juice, wine or vinegar before cooking.

Pork and vegetable ragoût

Cooking time: 45 minutes
Preparation time: 25 minutes
Main cooking utensils: 3 saucepans, 1-pint ($\frac{1}{2}$-litre) mould
Serves: 4–5

Imperial	Metric
8 oz. Brussels sprouts	200 g. Brussels sprouts
8 oz. carrots	200 g. carrots
4 oz. turnips	100 g. turnips
2 onions	2 onions
2 leeks	2 leeks
1 lb. lean pork, cut from leg or shoulder	$\frac{1}{2}$ kg. lean pork, cut from leg or shoulder
3 oz. butter or margarine	75 g. butter or margarine
1¼ pints chicken stock	625 ml. chicken stock
seasoning	seasoning
4 oz. long- or medium-grain rice	100 g. long- or medium-grain rice
6 large tomatoes	6 large tomatoes
2 teaspoons concentrated tomato purée	2 teaspoons concentrated tomato purée
$\frac{1}{2}$–1 teaspoon yeast or meat extract	$\frac{1}{2}$–1 teaspoon yeast or meat extract

1. Prepare the vegetables. Remove the outer leaves from sprouts, cut the peeled carrots and turnips into strips and the onions and leeks into thin slices.
2. Cut the pork into small pieces, season lightly.
3. Heat 2 oz. (50 g.) butter or margarine, toss the pork in it, add the vegetables and blend with the pork.
4. Stir in $\frac{3}{4}$ pint (375 ml.) of the stock, season and simmer steadily until the vegetables and meat are tender and the liquid absorbed.
5. Meanwhile, simmer the rice in the remainder of the stock until tender, and the liquid absorbed, about 15 minutes.
6. Simmer the skinned, deseeded tomatoes and the tomato purée with the remaining butter and add the yeast extract.
7. Put the tomato mixture into the mould, cover with the rice and leave in a warm place for a short time. Turn out and serve with the ragoût.

Curried cream kebabs

Cooking time: 20 minutes
Preparation time: 15 minutes
Main cooking utensils: 2 saucepans, grill pan, metal skewers
Serves: 6

Imperial	Metric
8 oz. long-grain rice	200 g. long-grain rice
$\frac{3}{4}$ pint water	375 ml. water
salt	salt
3 oz. butter	75 g. butter
1 oz. flour	25 g. flour
$\frac{1}{2}$–1 tablespoon curry powder	$\frac{1}{2}$–1 tablespoon curry powder
$\frac{1}{2}$ pint chicken stock	250 ml. chicken stock
$\frac{1}{4}$ pint thin cream	125 ml. thin cream
Kebabs:	*Kebabs:*
1 7-oz. can pork luncheon meat	1 198-g. can pork luncheon meat
6 rashers streaky bacon	6 rashers streaky bacon
1 green pepper	1 green pepper
1 onion	1 onion
1 small can pineapple chunks	1 small can pineapple chunks
4 oz. mushrooms	100 g. mushrooms
pepper	pepper
finely chopped parsley	finely chopped parsley

1. Put the rice, water and a good pinch of salt into a saucepan, bring the water to the boil, stir briskly, cover the pan and allow to simmer for 15 minutes.
2. Meanwhile melt 2 oz. (50 g.) butter, stir in the flour and curry powder and cook for 2–3 minutes.
3. Gradually blend in the stock, bring to the boil, cover the pan and simmer for nearly 15 minutes; add the cream just before serving.
4. For the kebabs, cut the luncheon meat into 1$\frac{1}{2}$-inch (4-cm.) cubes, and remove the rinds from the bacon, then halve each rasher and roll up.
5. Dice the green pepper, discard the core and seeds.
6. Peel the onion and cut into pieces.
7. Drain the pineapple, and wash and dry the mushrooms.
8. Put all the kebab ingredients alternately on to six metal skewers; melt the remaining butter, season and use to brush the kebabs.
9. Cook under a hot grill until the bacon and vegetables are cooked, turning once or twice.
10. Put the rice in a bowl, top with chopped parsley and the kebabs. Serve the sauce separately.

Onions stuffed with minced meat

Cooking time: approximately 1½ hours
Preparation time: 25 minutes
Main cooking utensils: saucepan, frying pan, ovenproof dish
Oven temperature: moderately hot (375°F., 190°C., Gas Mark 5)
Oven position: centre
Serves: 6

Imperial	Metric
6 large onions	6 large onions
seasoning	seasoning
4 oz. mushrooms (mushroom stalks can be used for economy)	100 g. mushrooms (mushroom stalks can be used for economy)
6 oz. bacon	150 g. bacon
2 oz. butter	50 g. butter
12 oz. minced beef, lamb or pork	300 g. minced beef, lamb or pork
good pinch powdered sage or little chopped fresh sage	good pinch powdered sage or little chopped fresh sage
2 oz. white or brown breadcrumbs	50 g. white or brown breadcrumbs
1 egg	1 egg
2 tablespoons chopped parsley or chervil	2 tablespoons chopped parsley or chervil
Sauce:	*Sauce:*
1½ oz. butter	40 g. butter
1 oz. flour	25 g. flour
just under ½ pint brown stock	250 ml. brown stock
¼ pint onion stock	125 ml. onion stock

1. Peel the onions and cook steadily in boiling, salted water for 15 minutes until the centres can be removed.
2. Take these out and chop finely.
3. Peel and chop the mushrooms, dice the bacon.
4. Heat the butter, fry the mushrooms and bacon in hot butter, add the chopped onion centres and meat. Cook for about 5—10 minutes, stirring well.
5. Add the remaining ingredients, using half the parsley or chervil only.
6. Season well, then press into the centres of the onions.
7. Make the sauce by heating the butter and stirring in the flour. Cook for several minutes, then gradually add the stock.
8. Bring to the boil, cook until thickened, pour into the dish.
9. Put the onions into the dish. Cover and cook for about 45 minutes, remove the lid and cook for a further 15 minutes.
10. Garnish with the remaining parsley or chervil.

Braised beef and vegetables

Cooking time: 2 hours
Preparation time: 25 minutes
Main cooking utensil: large saucepan with tightly fitting lid
Serves: 4—5

Imperial	Metric
8–10 medium-sized onions	8–10 medium-sized onions
1 lb. carrots	½ kg. carrots
8–12 oz. turnips or swedes	200–300 g. turnips or swedes
1½ lb. good quality stewing beef	¾ kg. good quality stewing beef
1½ oz. flour	40 g. flour
2 teaspoons paprika (see note)	2 teaspoons paprika (see note)
seasoning	seasoning
2 oz. fat	50 g. fat
1 pint brown stock	500 ml. brown stock
½ pint sour cream or yoghurt	250 ml. sour cream or yoghurt

1. Peel the onions, but leave them whole; peel the carrots and cut into slices and peel the turnips or swedes and cut into neat pieces.
2. Cut the meat into neat dice and coat with the flour, blended with paprika and plenty of seasoning.
3. Heat the fat and fry the onion, then add the meat and fry until golden. Lift meat and vegetables out on to a plate and gradually add the stock to the pan.
4. Bring to the boil and cook until thickened.
5. Replace the onions, meat and half the carrots and turnips or swede pieces. Simmer steadily for about 1 hour.
6. Add the remaining carrots and turnips and continue cooking for a further 45 minutes.
7. Each portion can be topped with sour cream or yoghurt.

Note: Paprika is not a hot pepper, it is produced from ripe peppers and gives a sweet flavour to dishes.

Variation
Stir the sour cream or yoghurt and a few caraway seeds into the stew just before serving.

Meat and potato pie

Cooking time: 1 hour 10 minutes
Preparation time: 35 minutes (see also stage 5)
Main cooking utensils: saucepan, baking tray
Oven temperature: hot (425–450°F., 220–230°C., Gas Mark 7–8)
   then moderate to moderately hot (350–375°F.; 180–190°C.,
   Gas Mark 4–5)
Oven position: centre
Serves: 5–6

Imperial	Metric
1¼ lb. potatoes, weight when peeled	generous ½ kg. potatoes, weight when peeled
seasoning	seasoning
8 oz. cooked ham or other cooked meat	200 g. cooked ham or other cooked meat
6—8 oz. bacon	150—200 g. bacon
2 onions	2 onions
1—2 tomatoes	1—2 tomatoes
clove garlic (optional)	clove garlic (optional)
2 oz. butter	50 g. butter
few sardines (optional)	few sardines (optional)
Pastry:	*Pastry:*
10 oz. self-raising flour	250 g. self-raising flour
salt	salt
4 oz. butter	100 g. butter
1 lemon	1 lemon
1 egg	1 egg
Glaze:	*Glaze:*
beaten egg	beaten egg

1. Put the potatoes into boiling, well-seasoned water, cook for 8 minutes, drain and slice.

2. Mince or dice the ham and bacon, slice the peeled onions and tomatoes, crush the garlic.

3. Heat the butter, toss the vegetables in it, add the meat, season and cool. Add the flaked sardines for an unusual flavour.

4. To make the pastry, sieve the flour with the salt, rub in the butter, add the finely grated lemon rind and juice and bind with egg and water, if necessary.

5. Roll out; use two-thirds to line a pudding basin, put in the meat and potato mixture. Roll out most of the remaining pastry to make a lid, press over the filling, seal the edges well and put in a cool place for 1 hour.

6. Turn out on to a baking sheet, decorate with leaves of pastry and glaze with egg. Bake for approximately 30 minutes, then reduce the heat for a further 20—25 minutes. Serve with roast potatoes.

Potato ring cake

Cooking time: 50 minutes plus time for cooking potatoes
Preparation time: 20 minutes
Main cooking utensil: ring tin
Oven temperature: moderate to moderately hot (350–375°F., 180–190°C., Gas Mark 4–5)
Oven position: centre
Serves: 8–10

Imperial	Metric
4 oz. boiled potatoes	100 g. boiled potatoes
4 oz. butter or margarine	100 g. butter or margarine
4 oz. castor sugar	100 g. castor sugar
grated rind of 1 lemon	grated rind of 1 lemon
3 large eggs, separated	3 large eggs, separated
juice of $\frac{1}{2}$ lemon	juice of $\frac{1}{2}$ lemon
4 oz. plain flour	100 g. plain flour
1 level teaspoon baking powder	1 level teaspoon baking powder
Decoration:	*Decoration:*
sieved icing sugar	sieved icing sugar
halved cherries	halved cherries

1. Rub the potatoes through a sieve.
2. Cream the butter and sugar and grated lemon rind until soft and light.
3. Beat the egg yolks with the lemon juice.
4. Add the yolk mixture very gradually to the butter mixture, beating well each time.
5. Sift the flour with baking powder and mix with the potato.
6. Whisk the egg whites.
7. Add the potato mixture and egg whites to the rest of the ingredients, stir till blended.
8. Put the mixture into the greased and floured tin.
9. Bake for the time and temperature given until firm to the touch.
10. Cool the cake on a wire tray.
11. Dust with sieved icing sugar, decorate with halved cherries.

Note: When baking always check oven temperature with that recommended in your cooker instruction card or book.

Variation
Flavour with orange rind and juice instead of lemon.

Acknowledgements

The following photographs are by courtesy of:

Ayds Reducing Plan: pages 16, 20, 22
California Prune Advisory Bureau: page 30
Champignon Käsewerk Limited (Germany): page 60
Danish Food Centre: pages 100, 118
Dutch Fruit and Vegetable Producers' Association: pages 12, 92, 116
Eden Vale: page 18
Fruit Producers' Council: pages 34, 108
Karl Ostmann Limited (Germany): pages 42, 48, 56, 76, 114
Kraft Foods Limited: page 8
Lard Information Bureau: pages 72, 112
Potato Marketing Board: page 82
Stork Cookery Service: page 58